Cashflow Reengineering

Cashflow Reengineering

How to Optimize the Cashflow Timeline and Improve Financial Efficiency

James S. Sagner

American Management Association

New York • Atlanta • Boston • Chicago • Kansas City • San Francisco • Washington, D.C.
Brussels • Mexico City • Tokyo • Toronto

Library of Congress Cataloging-in-Publication Data
Sagner, James S.
    Cashflow reengineering : how to optimize the cashflow timeline and
improve financial efficiency / by James S. Sagner.
       p.   cm.
    Includes index.
    ISBN 0–8144–0361–1
    1. Cash management.   2. Cash flow.   3. Corporations—Cash
position.   4. Cash management—United States—Case studies.
I. Title
HG4028.C45S23   1997
658.15′244—dc21   97–3861
                                                                CIP

Printing number
10 9 8 7 6 5 4 3 2 1

For Stephen and Jennifer, Amy and Scott, and Robert-Paul and Nadya

CONTENTS

Preface

This book grew out of my reaction to the recent explosion of interest in organizational reengineering, both in the business sector and in not-for-profit sectors such as governments and hospitals. Most organizational reengineering seemed to be making a fundamental mistake by focusing on one or the other of the two narrow paths.

The first path sees reengineering as redefining jobs, tasks, or management—without much analysis or methodology:

Start with a clean piece of paper and redesign how work is done.

The second path of reengineering is downsizing:

We need to save $10 million, which is equivalent to 250 jobs. Find 250 people we can do without, reassign their work, and tell the survivors to be grateful that their names aren't on the list—this time.

Both of these approaches to reengineering are a sham. The first provides no methodology or procedures to get from here to there, and the second makes no sincere attempt to retain the human beings who are the very reason any organization exists in the first place.

There is a third path, and that is the reason for this book. *Cashflow Reengineering* offers clear methods and procedures for improving organizational efficiency *without* slashing jobs.

The reengineering techniques presented here focus on the one asset every organization must have to survive: cash. We discuss ways to improve the management of cash both *within* the structure of the enterprise, and by *outsourcing.* In so doing, we provide opportunities to save that $10 million without firing 250 people.

My partners and I are now in our third decade of working with global corporations. Our consulting practice has taken us to organizations throughout North America, Europe, and the Far East. We have served industries and nonprofits including all levels of government and other institutions, and all types of manufacturing, retailing, and service industries. Our common thread with all of these organizations has been cash, and our goal has been to develop state-of-the-art financial systems and procedures for its management and use.

We are indebted to our clients for teaching us so much about how organizations really work. Textbook management— even case studies—means little when you walk into a living, breathing group of managers and workers hoping to do their best for themselves, their coworkers, their managers, and their ultimate bosses—their shareholders. We've learned that the best intentions in the world are also meaningless when walls are built around each function and subfunction so the people in Division A of Group I in Building 3 don't have a clue to what the people in Division B of Group II in Building 4 are doing.

Cashflow reengineering can succeed only if these attitudes change. Sadly, they are pervasive in many of the organizations in North America and Europe (but less so in the Far East). Psychologists tell us that behaviors change when it is too painful, too inefficient, or too risky to continue them. As many of us are aware, we may be reaching that point—a point where the attitudes *must* change or jobs and possibly entire organizations will vanish. We can start the change with the thoughtful application of the ideas in this book, particularly the OPQR paradigm described in Chapter 11.

I gratefully acknowledge the permission granted by the following publications for the use of material that originally appeared in their pages in somewhat different formats.

For material in Chapter 3: "Re-engineering Treasury Management Functions: Theory and Application", *TMA Journal* (formerly *Journal of Cash Management*), Nov.–Dec. 1994, Vol. 14. ©1994 by the Treasury Management Association, all rights reserved.

For material in Chapter 4: "A Formalized Approach to Purchasing Cash Management Services," *Journal of Cash Management*, Nov.–Dec. 1993, Vol. 13. ©1993 by the Treasury Management Association, all rights reserved. This material was substantially reworked for *Standardized RFPs*, published by the TMA and the Bank Administration Institute in 1996.

For material in Chapter 5: "Treasury Enters the Arena of Cost, Pricing and Profit Analysis," *Corporate Cashflow*, June 1996, Vol. 17. © 1996 by Argus Inc., all rights reserved.

For materials in Chapter 8: "Sharpen Cash Forecasts by Using Operations Data," *Corporate Cashflow*, April 1996, Vol. 17. © 1996 by Argus Inc., all rights reserved.

Certain material throughout this book originally appeared, beginning in 1994, in our quarterly newsletter, *Treasury Views.*

We thank our friends in financial positions throughout the globe for their loyalty and support through the years. Special friends include two bankers: Christopher Skaar, Jr., of First Chicago/NBD Bank, and Daniel Streiff, of the Bank of Montreal/Harris Bank. Four corporate friends are James McAuley, formerly of Aetna Life & Casualty and now of ITT The Hartford; Louis Patria, formerly of Travelers Insurance; Ronald Quist of Equitable Insurance; and Edward Banas, of DLJ/Pershing. Others are Ayo Mseka of the Treasury Management Association, Steve Maier of UAI/Phoenix-Hecht, and Tony De Caux of the Bank Relationship Consultancy (London). A particular thanks to Ken Atchity and David Angsten of Atchity Editorial/Entertainment International, Inc.

Many thanks to the Sagner/Marks partners, particularly Erik Bodow, for their patience during the writing of this book. For any errors of omission or commission, the blame is entirely mine.

chapter

•1•

The Reengineering of Organizations

Faith *is the substance of things hoped for, the evidence of things not seen.*
—The Epistle of Paul the Apostle to the Hebrews, 11:1

Faith *may be defined briefly as an illogical belief in the occurrence of the improbable.*
—H. L. Mencken (1880–1956)

We have all seen the numbers. AT&T eliminates 40,000 jobs out of a total of 123,000. Lockheed cuts 15,000 jobs from a total of 30,000. And it's not just an American phenomenon: The merger of the Swiss pharmaceutical firms Sandoz and Ciba-Geigy will cut 14,000 jobs from their global workforce. Other companies eliminate workers gradually and quietly so that the pain and notoriety are not as pronounced.

Many of us wonder if we're next on the list to be eliminated. The social and economic transformations driving the reengineering of organizations throughout the world have caused the loss of more than two million American jobs in the past five years, with further changes and reductions inevitable. What has caused this development? Are there alternative methods to make companies and other organizations more efficient?

The premise of this book is that organizations can be made more efficient *without* the wholesale elimination of people. Reengineering, the concept of redesigning an organization to save costs and time and to improve service, attempts to determine and implement more efficient business processes. (The pioneering work in this field is by Michael Hammer and James Champy in their book, *Reengineering the Corporation*, New York: HarperBusiness, 1993.) Certainly those improved processes may require the elimination of some jobs, but they can also involve elements of the expense structure of an organization that have largely been ignored.

Our consulting work with several hundred organizations over the past 15 years has been keyed to *cash*. By focusing on the information and decisions that are tied to cash (or the older term, *liquidity*), we have saved corporations hundreds of millions of dollars annually. The procedures presented in this book were developed for the largest international organizations, including some 200 of the Fortune 500 companies and numerous large public organizations including governments, hospitals, and museums.

While job cuts contributed to these savings, they were only a small element (typically one-fourth). Much of the savings were derived from the reduction of *float*, which is money in the process of collection, disbursement, or other use. Other savings came from using lower-priced bank and vendor services, reducing internal operating costs (other than people costs), and from other efficiencies. This can be done in your organization, and we're going to show you how.

■ MANAGEMENT VOGUES AND FASHIONS

Business and management practices, forever changing and evolving, tend to develop in trends. In their pursuit of the current fashion, organizations often behave like lemmings: They follow each other into the sea regardless of whether going into the sea is a good idea.

After the First World War, the trend was "scientific management," pioneered by Frederick W. Taylor. The basis of scientific management was the time-and-motion study, which defined the precise method to accomplish each task and subtask; the time, tools, and training required; and the appropriate pay. Taylor's methods promised increased wages for workers and higher productivity for the corporation.

Another trend began in the 1930s. Largely through the work of Elton Mayo at the Hawthorne plant of Western Electric, companies came to realize that the employee might have important input into the structure of his or her job. "Human relations" management became the fashion.

During the 1960s, the buzzwords were "self-actualization" (Abraham Maslow) and "hygiene factors" (Frederick Herzberg). Organizations began to believe that money, wages, and a job were insufficient motivators. Maslow developed his theory of the "hierarchy of needs," with employees pursuing successively higher levels of gratification: physiological (or basic) needs, security (or safety) needs, social (belonging to the work group) needs, ego (or self-esteem) needs, and self-actualization (self-fulfillment) needs. Herzberg believed that basic work elements—company policies, wages, working conditions—were only capable of being "dissatisfiers" (when unfulfilled), and that satisfaction could only come through recognition, achievement, and a sense of responsibility.

In order to keep up with their competitors in the 1970s, companies bought mainframe computers, even though most had no specific applications under development and limited programming or systems support. It wasn't until the computers were installed that management considered their functionality. Systems analysts and programmers were hired, and computer companies made massive profits from continually upgrading hardware capacity.

Today, in the age of instant communications, the trend is to track other companies' activities and performance, assess

Wall Street's reaction, and then adapt the best and often the worst of these activities for their own organizations. Companies today are keenly aware of the perception of their potential performance by the investment banking community and are anxious to do everything in their power to increase shareholder value. Not-for-profit organizations are also under the microscope of public scrutiny, and charities and governments are cutting expenses, eliminating marginal services, and enhancing their value to contributors and taxpayers.

Managers and other workers are caught in the middle of these pressures. Their jobs may be eliminated as organizations struggle to meet expectations. Companies failing to make forecast earnings are often subject to harsh treatment by the equity markets in the form of severe declines in the company's stock price. While the nonprofit sector may not be subject to such extreme discipline, government and charitable organizations that fail to efficiently accomplish their missions are subject to close scrutiny by their overseers, whether it be Congress, a board of directors or trustees, or another group.

The difference between the fashions of the past and today's reengineering/downsizing mania is that—for the first time in an economy that is not in a depression—there is widespread job elimination. Earlier trends were relatively harmless: Managers and workers retained their jobs while senior executives tinkered with the production process and the organizational structure. In some cases, results did actually improve!

What are the factors driving the current trend of reengineering and downsizing?

- *Overcapacity leads to cost reductions.* Technology and the globalization of markets have produced far more goods and services than can be absorbed in our present low-growth economy. (For example, it is estimated that there are only seven buyers for every ten automobiles now produced.) Deregulation and free trade eliminate artificial market barriers and allow companies to produce for sale in new markets worldwide.

  In the United States, industries formerly constrained or protected by governmental barriers—banking, public utilities, transportation, communications, oil, insurance—are now either entirely competitive or evolving toward competition. As trade barriers fall, prices seek market levels established by the global market instead of cost-plus levels set by government fiat. With market and profit protection going or gone, earnings can only be sustained by working smarter or eliminating expenses. This situation appears irreversible for the forseeable future.

- *Employees are identifiable cost elements.* Workers are discrete cost units whose identities are easily determined. It is much simpler to determine potential cost savings from the elimination of a selected number of managers than it is to develop savings by internal improvements through outsourcing or other reengineering strategies.

  These efforts require comprehensive knowledge of how a business process works, the analysis of that process, and the quantification of alternative approaches. With the compartmentalizing of jobs into strategic business units (SBUs) and functions, most managers have no broad perspective on their organization. Making it operate better is certainly much harder work than simply eliminating jobs to save dollars.

  Executives are constantly prodded by consultants and stock market analysts to become more efficient. If they refuse and earnings disappoint the markets, the company's stock price can be driven down 10–20 percent in a single day's trading. When the decision is finally made to cut, say, $25 million from annual costs, it is much easier to downsize by 1,000 jobs ($25 million divided by an assumed $25,000 per employee) than to save $25 million through reengineering.

- *Management's role has diminished.* The textbook definition of *management* includes decision making, assembling elements of production, and providing strategic direction. Since the 1970s, however, most managers spend their time collecting and analyzing data and preparing reports about significant exceptions to plans and targets. They also administer regulations, from occupational safety to equal employment opportunity to environmental issues. They spend time on energy conservation, product safety, and a host of other concerns that relate only indirectly to the mission of the enterprise.

The impact of the manager on the making and selling of product has clearly diminished. This phenomenon has sometimes been referred to as "the death of middle management." Grand strategy, assembling the elements of production, and decision making—these are the domain of senior executives. Information technology has simplified the assembly of data, and the need for managers, except to respond to governmental regulation, has been significantly reduced.

■ *Managers are expensive.* In selecting employees for downsizing, obviously the cost of each worker is a major consideration. Managers have been higher paid than technical or skilled personnel throughout the life of the modern corporation, but particularly since the installation of quantitative job evaluation and compensation systems (see Robert M. Tomasko, *Downsizing, Reshaping the Corporation for the Future*, New York: AMACOM, 1990). Points assigned to jobs are based on the technical and managerial skills and the training and education required; compensation is based on total points awarded. In addition, managers are often financially rewarded for the performance of their business units, resulting in higher compensation for them than for other employees. This makes everyone to want to be a manager, and more managerial positions are created to accommodate workers deemed critical to the success of the organization.

■ WHAT ARE THE RESULTS OF REENGINEERING AND DOWNSIZING?

The widespread dismissal of managers and workers to meet the profitability expectations of Wall Street has had a variety of unfortunate consequences. The nature of these consequences depends in large part on the specific structure of the organization.

Many organizations have developed a decentralized strategic business unit (SBU) or profit-center structure, with specific goals and profitability expectations for each business unit. Typically, each unit is provided with the assets it needs to function: capital, equipment, people, product development resources, systems support, and salespeople. The unit manager organizes these resources as best he or she can, has successes and failures, learns from these experiences, and generally carries forward the business mission of the corporation.

Other businesses, primarily those offering fewer product lines or less geographically dispersed operations, utilize a more centralized, functional form of organization. Here managers may be responsible for a portion of a large production or marketing function. This structural form usually offers less autonomy to managers, but has the advantage of a more focused control over the activities of the business. It also avoids the duplication of functional activities that occurs in a corporation with numerous SBUs. According to Alfred Chandler (*Strategy and Structure*, Cambridge: MIT Press, 1962), the optimal organizational form (the structure) follows the grand strategy selected.

When downsizing occurs and managers are eliminated, resources are either reassigned to other uses and purposes or left to drift. Many reengineering survivors, who once were part of a team of managers and workers, are now expected to either conduct the business of the new team or accept reassignment to other responsibilities. How do they react to this?

- *Survivor guilt.* During a corporate downsizing, much of the energy of the workforce is diverted to speculation about personnel decisions by the organization. Who will stay and who will go become far more important issues than "Can we ship on time?" or "Can we sell enough product?" Many survivors are paralyzed by feelings of guilt that they were spared while their coworkers were not. This guilt frequently results in lasting emotional distress, including uncontrollable crying, depression, and difficulty in concentrating on daily tasks. And often the distress is exacerbated because the survivor expects that his or her status will change the next time, as inevitably seems to occur in many large organizations.

  It's not hard to imagine that focusing on global strategy will become secondary to worrying about personal survival. Few survivors will champion new products or programs, and organizational initiative is often destroyed.

The prevailing attitude may change from developing new ideas and approaches to problems to "hunkering down" in order to not be seen.

- *Sabotage.* Managers and workers may believe that an un-written "social contract" exists between the employer and themselves, which states that a lifetime job is guaranteed as long as the employee continues to exert all necessary effort for the success of the enterprise. Downsizing often eliminates jobs en masse, without regard for the efforts of specific employees, their length of service, their loyalty, or other factors. The resulting anger of the terminated employee may lead to attempts at sabotage. This may include the destruction of files, records, and orders; theft; refusal to complete required tasks; adverse comments to the news media and to customers; and other negative actions. Sometimes the saboteur is the survivor—if he or she is not too despondent to act!

  Companies are often advised to require terminated employees to leave the premises immediately so that the opportunity for sabotage is limited. In those situations, outplacement facilities and counseling may be made available through employment agencies. Other organizations place reengineered workers in a special office area that is part of the physical premises of the company. This allows them to pursue new positions while ostensibly employed by the downsizing firm.

- *Experience gap.* The dismissal of managers inevitably includes those with long service in the organization who have seen and can help solve the unusual problem or know where vital resources can be found. These workers are often included in the downsizing because their salaries are higher than more junior employees, or because a strategic decision has been made to reduce or eliminate particular SBUs. Without the knowledge base that these experienced people provide, the organization often muddles along at a less than efficient rate.

- *Political maneuvering.* Managers and workers seeking to advance their careers commonly develop political alliances with bosses and peers in hopes of receiving favorable treatment. During downsizing, the maneuvering to ally with executives in power can become the primary task of work, more than producing and selling widgets or making a profit. The perception that influence or favored treatment may mitigate termination can cause the mission of the organization to be overwhelmed by political activity.

Given these reactions to downsizing, how can the organization successfully continue toward the accomplishment of its mission?

■ CAN REENGINEERING ACCOMPLISH ITS OBJECTIVES?

Much of the significant promise of reengineering remains unfulfilled. In *Reengineering Management* (New York: Harper Business, 1995), Champy admitted that goals set in specific reengineering efforts failed by as much as 30 percent and that "the revolution we started has gone, at best, only halfway. I have also learned that half a revolution is not better than none. It may, in fact, be worse" (p. 3).

Here are some outcomes from the reengineering revolution observed in our own consulting work:

- The manufacturing process of a **consumer durable goods** company was reengineered to reduce production time and inventories and improve gross margins. The project involved integrating separate SBUs and eliminating certain redundant functions, including some personnel and overhead. The project failed when the vice presidents of the SBUs realized that their independence was being threatened and that cooperation toward the common mission would be required.

- A diversified **financial services** company had several investment departments in various locations, none of which was of sufficient size to warrant independent operations. The company was advised to integrate the investment departments and to develop economies by maintaining self-contained bond and equity trading floors and a comprehensive cash forecasting operation. The recommendation was ignored because the investment function had previously provided large returns to the company and it was unwilling to consider an alternative plan.

- An international **aviation** company considered reengineering its parts distribution system in order to decrease the number of locations and employees and to concurrently lessen inventory held awaiting sales. The project required that the senior executive of the distribution business agree to eliminate portions of his "empire" and to be counseled by outsiders (consultants) regarding optimal surviving locations and inventory. The project failed because of his resistance.

In each of these cases, the failure of the reengineering effort led to far more radical actions. The consumer durable goods company eventually moved the entire production process to another country, citing lower manufacturing costs. This resulted in the loss of 2,000 jobs and the closing of the SBUs. The financial services company was absorbed in a takeover, and new senior management was brought in. The investment groups and numerous other businesses were eliminated, with the loss of 10,000 jobs. The aviation company's board of directors fired senior management, including the chief executive officer, and sold parts of the company to a competitor.

Cases like these have several themes in common:

- *Self-preservation.* Managers and workers do not willingly cooperate to reengineer a process when their authority and prestige are threatened. Appeals to the mission of the organization or the common good are often useless, and even if agreed to, may be subverted by covert acts of resistance.

- *Refusal to change.* Managers and workers are comfortable with the processes they know and uneasy about change. When ordered to comply, "shadow" or parallel systems and procedures often arise to accomplish the work.

- *Resistance to advice.* It is an iron rule that consultants are distrusted and ignored in many organizations. Managers and workers tend to resist any advice from those perceived to be outsiders on the grounds that only SBU personnel can be the experts in their business. This principle holds true even within the organization when staff (advisory) personnel attempt to counsel line employees, those directly responsible for production and marketing.

The clear lesson is that when employees believe that their interests lie in preserving the status quo, they're likely to resist the reengineering of their work or their organization. The challenge, discussed throughout this book, is to gain acceptance for positive change without the drastic surgery of downsizing or the sale of the business.

■ THE CASHFLOW REENGINEERING SOLUTION

There is now a growth industry in reengineering consulting and publishing—and, unfortunately, in the strategy of eliminating jobs to make financial results attractive for shareholders and other constituent groups. The popular literature in this field generally provides various platitudes and cases illustrating how to or how not to do reengineering. The constant refrain, however, is that no two situations are the same and that the process is very difficult.

The problem is that these reengineering books provide little information on specific procedures to use in this work. No generalized methodology has been developed. The most glaring flaw may be the attempt to explain "lessons" from specific cases. Many different disciplines are involved in a reengineering effort (finance, production, systems, accounting) making any lesson difficult to apply from Organization A to Organization B. One writer, after suggesting that a major mistake is to overanalyze the organization's existing processes, devoted an entire chapter to the process of selecting a consultant! Apparently, no executive could be clever enough to manage that process on his or her own.

Our message is clearly different: Cashflow reengineering is not voodoo, it is not a mystery. When evaluating a cashflow reengineering plan, there are a limited number of alternatives to consider and specific analytical processes to help you choose the right one. The choice is determined by a quantitative measurement—cash—a specific amount of which can be saved if the proposed changes are made. Estimates of potential benefits are based on proposed internal improvements and/or outsourcing. Measurements are fairly precise: the value of float *or* the savings between the current process and the alternative. In our experience, senior executives and middle managers accept such reengineering recommendations for a number of reasons:

- *Large attainable savings.* A good example is outsourcing disbursements to a bank (see Chapter 7), which can save $1.50 or more per paper transaction. A company issuing 5,000 checks monthly can save nearly $100,000 each year. Banks and vendors will already have the service in place with numerous current clients, and implementation time is usually only three or four months. Perhaps most important, there's no built-in opposition to this decision, because no one SBU is totally responsible for the check disbursement function. Exhibit 1-1 illustrates other examples of cashflow reengineering savings from internal improvements and outsourcing.

- *No massive job losses.* In our disbursement outsourcing example, the savings are derived from eliminating inefficient internal processes, including the costs of mainframe computer time, preprinted checkstock, bursting and signing, first-class postage, and internal check reconciliation. Most important, the savings from lost jobs would only be about 25 percent of the total, equivalent to one person (considering wages and fringe benefits).

  There is no surer path to destroying morale and producing failure than to eliminate large numbers of jobs. The social contract is destroyed and the concept of an organizational mission is compromised. The experiences cited in Exhibit 1-1 involved limited job elimination and, certainly, no loss of the organizational work ethic. If anything, the competitive desire to compete and win was enhanced at each company.

- *No theory or faith requiring a "religious" acceptance.* Throughout reengineering literature, there is a recurring idea of dependence on faith. One reference states that the

Industry	Annual Sales ($ millions)	Annual Savings	Significant Cashflow Reengineering Changes and Book Chapter Discussion*
	EXHIBIT 1-1 Illustrative Cashflow Reengineering Savings (based on results with consulting clients)		
Aero-space	$10,000	$7,200,000	Review gross margin and profitability analysis (5) End early release of accounts payable checks (7)
Bakery pro-ducts	400	$250,000	Close branch imprest cash and bank balances (6) Deposit daily all walked-in payments (6)
Building equip-ment	1,700	$390,000	Change lockbox locations (6) Use cash discounts and late interest charges to improve cash collections (9)
Consu-mer pro-ducts	1,000	$400,000	Use procurement cards for small purchases (7) Improve forecasting of daily cash position (8)
Health care	80	$300,000	Centralize purchasing to attain volume discounts (7) Use EDI for collections and disbursements (6, 7)
Mortgage bank-ing	1,800	$1,300,000	Reduce size of short-term investment pool (8) Determine optimal structure of financing (9)
Oil and gas	400	$250,000	Pay bank charges by fees rather than balances (8) Renegotiate bank prices for certain bank services (8)
Power gener-ation	700	$150,000	Establish lockbox for corporate utility payments (6) Review cash concentration procedures (8)

EXHIBIT 1-1 Continued			
Industry	**Annual Sales ($ millions)**	**Annual Savings**	**Significant Cashflow Reengineering Changes and Book Chapter Discussion***
Public utility	2,000	$550,000	Encourage individuals to pay by ACH debits (7) For mailed payments, schedule bank courier for a later deposit pick-up (6)
Scientific equip-ment	1,200	$600,000	Increase direct deposit of payroll (7) Close cash imprest account; negotiate for ATMs (7)
Stocks & bonds	(Assets) 25,000	$16,500,000	Fix late billing of trade confir-mations to customers (6) Use "Positive Pay" for branch disbursements to prevent fraud (7)

*Discussion of reengineering opportunity is located in this chapter

proper approach is not to reengineer *work*—the opera-tions or tasks performed by managers and workers—but to reengineer *management*, the process of organizing and directing scarce resouces (such as land, labor, and capi-tal) into a productive enterprise. We claim that the reengi-neering of a work process will fail unless the manager's attitude supervising that work process is also reengi-neered (see Champy, *Reengineering Management*).

Attitude adjustment is for psychiatrists, psychologists, and bartenders. The goal in this book, and your job, is to develop the optimal process to accomplish a work task, including assembling the necessary resources. As in our disbursement outsourcing example, no faith or psychol-ogy is required. The banks/vendors bid on the service, and you accept or decline. A consultant can analyze your internal costs and can assist with the selection from alternative bidders, but there's no reason you can't get there yourself with a little effort.

■ MANAGING CASH AND CREATING CUSTOMERS

Changes are occuring in organizations of all types and sizes—not just to the AT&Ts and Lockheeds of the world. The purpose of this book is to assist managers in *any* company to do a better job of assembling their resources and becoming more efficient. We make a thorough examination of banking and vendor services and explore a variety of ways to improve existing internal processes.

Shakespeare's fiery warrior Hotspur, on the eve of battle with the armies of King Henry IV, spoke of "the very life-blood of our enterprise" (*King Henry the Fourth*, Part I, act IV, sc. i). In addition to your efforts to create customers and emphasize quality, we want you to focus on CASH as the lifeblood of *your* enterprise.

We begin in Chapter 2 with a discussion of cashflow reengineering and management principles. It is essential that *all* managers understand these basic principles because, in the traditional workflow of a corporation, no *one* manager has direct responsibility for cashflow, even though it's the organization's most critical asset. Several popular systems for defining business objectives have made the evaluation of business and managerial performance confusing; we explain why cashflow reengineering is the appropriate goal for any organization.

Chapter 3 explains how the careful analysis of current processes is a necessary first step to establish a benchmark for potential changes. The next step is to determine if internal improvements are feasible or if the process should be outsourced. Chapter 4 discusses the outsourcing alternative, while Chapters 5 through 9 address various internal improvements. Chapter 10 reviews risk management and control procedures, and Chapter 11 outlines the OPQR paradigm of management, as a summary.

■ ■ ■

CHAPTER 1 APPENDIX
PROCEDURES FOR THE ANALYSIS AND IMPROVEMENT OF CASHFLOW ACTIVITIES

Documentation of the major cashflows of an organization begins with a series of tiered interviews, during which managers at successively lower levels of the organization are interviewed to determine the specific details of how each flow is handled. Flowcharting techniques can be used to depict the movement of treasury and related information flows graphically for each discrete treasury flow. The flowcharts can be supported by narratives that describe elements of the flowcharts in detail and provide bank account numbers or accounting ledger codes, levels of business activity, and other pertinent information. This documentation process serves three purposes:

1. Flowcharts are valuable analytical tools that facilitate the identification of illogical or inefficient cash/information flows.
2. Current system statistics provide a baseline for evaluating possible change.
3. The documentation can be used for internal training purposes and can facilitate communication among the various organizational entities that impact a treasury flow.

The cashflow documentation, various written procedures, and bank reports can be analyzed to identify opportunities for improvement. These can include streamlining existing procedures, introducing new technology including financial information systems, consolidating activities, changing the timing of cashflows, shifting between in-house and bank or vendor processing, and negotiating lower bank/vendor prices. In developing improvement ideas, it is important to take into account standard practices and trends as well as knowledge of current developments in financial management.

Recommendations resulting from these analyses generally include descriptions of each idea, a summary of facts supporting the idea, an estimate of the potential benefits, expected implementation costs, estimated implementation difficulty, and a list of open issues that must be resolved prior to implementation. A good procedure is to attempt to gain an early victory with those recommendations requiring minimal implementation time, to develop organizational support, to successfully demonstrate that real savings are attainable, and to "seed" or fund more complex changes involving significant investment.

Computer modeling can be used to support various analyses. Models are available to simulate the float environment in collection and disbursement systems, the pattern of check clearing at commercial banks, the pricing by banks and vendors for financial products, and bank balance management. The models for float simulation and check clearing and the databases that drive the analysis are marketed by UAI/Phoenix-Hecht of Research Triangle Park, NC.

Pricing for Financial Products and Bank Balance Management

There are models available that review the charges of banks and vendors for financial products, and that can analyze the management of bank balances. Significant savings can be developed through reduced bank/vendor service charges, elimination of balance compensation to banks and payment of charges in fees, and the evaluation of effective earnings credit rates (versus rates stated by banks on their invoices known as "account analyses").

Benefits are derived from calculations and comparative analysis of the service charges of clients by operating product for each bank/vendor. In addition, the opportunity costs of bank compensation in relation to service charge balances, excess balances, and effective earnings credit rates are determined and presented in a comparative analytical format. Nearly all input data is derived from vendor statements. The models interpret the input, comparatively array service fees, and analyze the status of balances used for services and free balances. Models of bank pricing and balance management are available from several treasury consulting firms, including Sagner/Marks.

chapter

· 2 ·

Cashflow Reengineering and Management Principles

*The **Goal** of life is living in agreement with nature.*

—Zeno (335–263 B.C.)

*My **object** all sublime*
I shall achieve in time
To let the punishment fit the crime.

—Sir W. S. Gilbert (1836–1911)

Cash is the essential element in any business. Cashflow reengineering focuses on the movement of cash through your organization and the information and events connected to it. This movement of cash in, through, and out of the organization is called the *cashflow timeline* (Exhibit 2-1). Careful examination of the timeline can reveal areas where internal processing can be improved, as well as indicate areas where outsourcing to vendors, particularly banks, would be more efficient. Financial management techniques are used to reconfigure events along the timeline, including:

- Time value of money ("present value")
- Gross margin analysis
- Scenario impact analysis
- A formalized bidding procedure for outsourcing

Cashflow reengineering improves income statement and cash position by maximizing operating results and managerial performance. While it does address various balance sheet accounts, it does *not* restructure the balance sheet through the use of bank credit instruments, public debt, or equity. Obvi-

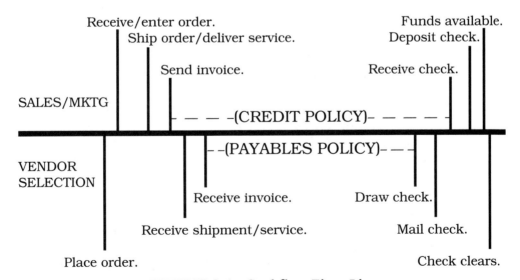

EXHIBIT 2-1 Cashflow Time Line

ously, a strong financial position directly correlates with access to credit and equity markets, but it's our experience that modern organizations must improve the former before expecting lenders and investors to participate in the risks and rewards of a business. (We use the term "business" in its older, traditional sense of any purposeful activity or endeavor, referring to not-for-profit organizations as well as for-profit corporations).

In addition to examining the cashflow timeline, this chapter introduces six of a total of **Ten Management Principles** that explain organizational behaviors that lead to business problems. Principles 7 through 10 are discussed in the next chapter. In Chapter 11, these principles are consolidated into four basic themes:

- The Organizational performance, or "O" problem

- The analytical Process, or "P" problem

- The Quantification, or "Q" problem

- The financial Reengineering, or "R" solution

Improvements in an organization's performance are functions of O, P, Q, and R, as we will demonstrate in Chapter 11 with cases drawn from our consulting experience.

■ THE "UNDERMANAGED" CASHFLOW TIMELINE

A typical organization, profit or not-for-profit, operates with two elements essential to all its activities: *cash* and *information*. Much of the information in any organization is connected with a cash event. Cash that is received or disbursed is usually preceded by information (an invoice for the sale of goods or services) or is followed by information (application of payment against an open receivable).

In the traditional division of corporate management—sales, manufacturing, finance, information systems—no one manager has direct responsibility for these cash and information activities. The only situation in which one manager may have such oversight is in a decentralized organization with many SBUs, and those organizations, as we shall see, have numerous other cash management problems. Most often the only common "manager" for all of the cash and information activities is the CEO or chief operating officer, who never, in our experience, has knowledge of or interest in the specific functioning of those activities. Yet as we noted at the conclusion of Chapter 1, cash is the lifeblood of any organization; it is arguably the most critical asset to those who depend on the survival of the business.

In order to better understand and analyze the cashflows in your organization, you can prepare a *payment stream matrix* listing cash/information flows by name, dollar volume, and manager (see Exhibit 2-2). The matrix becomes a kind of road map to understanding and improving your enterprise by indicating major cashflows and their mechanisms. A *cashflow* is defined as an activity of the organization that generates a cash inflow or outflow. Inflows, or collection flows, are usually derived from the sale of products or services; outflows, or disbursement flows, are payments to vendors for purchases (accounts payable), payroll, and other uses of cash. The term *mechanism* refers to the cash process normally used for the flow; each process will be fully described as it is encountered later in the book.

Constructing the payment stream matrix may require the help of personnel from various other disciplines within your organization. It's usually necessary to involve managers in all of the functional areas of the business, including sales, operations, and finance. It may also be important to include branch office personnel to account for transactions initiated in the field and sent on to headquarters for further processing. Even input from customers and vendors can be helpful; if you understand a transaction from all perspectives, you can make the process more efficient and effective for all parties.

Individual managers are often unaware of their impact on an organization's overall cashflow. Decisions about this most critical asset—cash—are often made without thoughtfully exploring the ramifications. Let's take a look at how this can occur:

- *Insurance company premiums.* According to various studies by Sagner/Marks and by other large companies, the

EXHIBIT 2-2 Payment Stream Matrix				
Name of Cashflow and Mechanism	**Managed Where?**	**Manager**	**Supervisor**	**Annual $ Volume**
1 Product W, Lockbox	Home Ops, Anytown	Rebecca Rhea	Sandy Sparrow	$500 million
2 Product X, Office Receipts	Division A, Anytown	Betty Bear	Charles Capybara	$250 million
3 Product Y, Wire Transfers	Division B, Anytown	Tony Tiger	Ursula Unicorn	$1.2 billion
4 Product Z, ACH Collections	Big Dept, Sometown	Wendy Walrus	Yetta Yak	$100 million
5 Accounts Payable, Check Disbursements	Large Dept, Sometown	Zachary Zebra	Anthony Alligator	$30 million
6 Accounts Payable, ACH Disbursements	Vivi Section, Yourtown	Denise Dolphin	Erik Eagle	$25 million
7 Payroll, Direct Deposit	Inter Section, Mytown	Frances Flounder	George Gopher	$80 million
8 Payroll, Check Disbursement	Grope Group, Ourtown	Harry Halibut	Ira Ibex	$75 million

best time to issue premium notices to encourage payment by the due date is 25 days prior to the due date; any deviation from that timing causes later payment. Despite this fact, one insurance company issued premium notices to individual and corporate policyholders *at times determined by access to the computer systems.* The decision on the premium notice date was based on factors bearing no relation to cashflow.

■ *Hospital purchases.* A not-for-profit hospital purchased supplies from various vendors and carefully cross-checked purchase orders with receiving reports to make certain that all materials were received as ordered. The only problem was that the invoices were paid as received and verified, without regard to either the due date or the customary payment practice in the industry. This resulted in early payment by an average of five days, costing the hospital hundreds of thousands of dollars every year.

These situations are typical of a narrow focus on minor objectives that may be at odds with the major goals of the enterprise. The insurance company was blindly focused on the convenience of the systems group, while the hospital was overly concerned with closing a vendor transaction (sometimes called the "clean desk" syndrome). We could cite numerous other examples of this managerial focus on the wrong organizational goals; the list is as varied as the functions and types of enterprises in the world.

> **Principle I.** Managers often focus on objectives that serve their management roles but fail to serve the major goals of their organizations.

■ FALLACIES IN DEFINING BUSINESS OBJECTIVES

The various systems of defining business and performance objectives are not without flaws. It's important to remember that none of these systems are incorrect, however; in fact, they may all be correct in different situations and at different times. For example, customer creation and profitability may sometimes conflict with one another, but they are excellent ideas and a business cannot long survive without them.

Nevertheless, several popular systems for defining business objectives have confused the task of evaluating business performance. The next few pages describe some of these systems and the flaws inherent in them.

Creating a Customer

For many years, the classic goal of the corporation was maximizing profits or return-on-equity. In 1954, Peter Drucker redefined the role to that of creating a customer (*The Practice of Management*, New York: Harper & Row). In his words, "[I]t is the customer, and he alone, who through being willing to pay for a good or for a service, converts economic resources into wealth, things into goods" (p. 37).

In some organizations customer creation has gone beyond the traditional sales or marketing divisions and become an objective for any business unit having customer contact. Broadly defined, this can mean anyone in the enterprise, because customers need service, customers have billing questions, and customers care about manufacturing quality. A good example of this can be seen in the consumer marketing approach of Saturn and General Motors, with their emphasis on total immersion with the customer throughout the automobile buying and owning cycle.

We all recognize that an enterprise cannot survive without the creation of customers, but we also know that sales without profits cannot be made up by volume. Many organizations, however, have so drastically segmented the responsibilities of managers that sales have become the only measure of success. For example, a commercial finance company evaluated certain managers primarily by the amount of business they wrote—basically a commission plan of compensation. This led to a situation in which nearly every sale was won by pricing below cost. The expectation that these losses would become profits in later years never occurred; pricing in later years remained as aggressive as in the year the service was first sold. Commissions, however, were huge, and the managers fought to protect the system.

In any sales function, of course, the focus is on the sale itself, not on the profit generated. Few businesses tie manufacturing, sales, and administrative costs to specific sales. Even fewer have any idea if a particular sale, product, or market generates appropriate threshold profits. Accounting of unit costs has historically been tied to production and not to marketing; the job of the accountant is to tell us to the tenth of a penny the cost to manufacture a "widget". It would be highly unusual for an organization to then tie that precise production cost to all of the other costs necessary to make the sale.

Personal objectives may also supersede the goals of the enterprise in situations other than sales. For example, one client of ours maintained a fleet of 1,500 automobiles for executives and managers and paid for expensive parking space in a major U.S. city. As long as an employee "warranted" that he or she drove more than 12,000 miles per year on company business (certifying that the vehicle was not used for personal activities), the benefit remained undisturbed. No systematic attempt was made to monitor vehicle use based on trip logs or other data, and comments in our consulting report regarding this "perk" were vigorously attacked by company management.

> **Principle II.** Managers often focus on *personal* objectives that undermine the major goals of their organizations.

Profitability

Profit is an important objective in any enterprise, but for a number of reasons it can have little meaning to the individual manager. The manager often has very imprecise data on which to judge the profitability of his or her product, service, or business line and little input to the process of assigning costs against revenues. Allocating nondirect organizational costs to specific SBUs is particularly difficult. Furthermore, although certain costs are variable in the long run and therefore subject to some control, nearly all costs are fixed in the short run. For example, labor is usually considered as a variable direct cost, yet hiring, transfer, and termination decisions are subject to fixed contractual and legislated restrictions.

Organizations can be sliced into any number of SBUs or profit centers, often solely on the whim of the senior executives. A bank can have an SBU for every service, every industry, and every geographic market served. Or it can have an SBU for aggregations of services, industries, and markets. Similarly, a manufacturing company can be separated into individual product groups or markets served or aggregated in various ways. There's nothing magical about the SBU/profit center format, however. It is often touch and feel, the result of historical accident, of a consultant's report, of executive political battles over turf, or of being forced to create management jobs for workers as a form of reward.

The measurement of SBU profitability can be taken to the extreme. Imagine, for example, a large corporation with 100 business units, each with its assignment of direct and indirect overhead. Any business units that fail to meet a target return-on-equity (ROE) is subject to elimination, on the theory that those units are a drag on enterprise results. The elimination of, say, 20 units, however, doesn't eliminate the overhead—except possibly in the very long run. Thus, the other 80 units receive a larger overhead allocation, some of them fail to meet the target ROE, and the cycle is repeated. Taken to its absurd conclusion, one SBU would remain and, of course, the enterprise would fail to meet the target return.

Realistically, the cycle stops when senior management discovers what is happening and rethinks the ROE criterion. This insight can take years, however, causing the loss of hundreds or thousands of jobs and significantly affecting the capability of the enterprise to offer an integrated package of goods and service to customers. For example, a large bank that, over time, reduced the number of its SBUs from 175 to about half of that number eliminated several SBUs that provided important but "low margin" services to corporations.

Recommendations to terminate SBUs are often made by staff or consultants not actively involved in customer contact. They fail to understand that customers buy "bundled" (rather than individual) products and services from their vendors. A business relationship involves numerous transactions that will hopefully earn an acceptable aggregate return. The vendor may lose money or break even on a few transactions due to price competition, but this is accepted for the sake of maintaining an overall profitable relationship. In the bank situation, several of its customers were forced to find other service providers, creating considerable ill will and the eventual termination of the relationship. Years will pass before those customers will return to the bank.

> **Principle III.** Objectives appropriate to the enterprise may be inappropriate to the individual business or functional unit.

Management by Objectives

Management by Objectives (MBO) is a popular managerial technique in which the manager develops quantifiable objectives in order to measure and track job performance. For example, an MBO might be to complete all analyses within three weeks of the receipt of files, to go on 50 sales calls, or to process 200 invoices a week. There are several problems with this approach:

- *Relevance of objective.* Achievement of the MBO can become an end in itself, without regard to changing business conditions and organizational priorities. Fifty sales calls may not be enough if they're not bringing in new business, or they may be unnecessary if several major contracts have already been made.

- *Quantity not quality.* The MBO measures quantity, but it doesn't measure the *quality* of performance. For example, a sales call can be perfunctory, five minutes long, made merely to count toward the MBO goal without any real exchange of information. Or it can be carefully planned, researched, and developed, with materials, a script, "leave-behinds" (such as a brochure), and follow-up (such as a "thank-you" letter). Should these two calls be counted as equivalent?

- *Validity of objectives.* Who knows if a set of MBOs is the right set of objectives, or if some nonquantifiable objective is more important to the success of the organization? A valid objective might be to do a better job managing people through work interaction, counseling, and advocating training. Yet none of these are easily measured, unless one counts the number of contacts or the number of minutes devoted to being a better manager.

- *Change in objectives.* During the course of a year, downsizing, reassignments, and new business initiatives may change management's allocation of resources. Many employees have had the experience of working diligently toward fulfillment of their MBOs, only to be asked to take on projects for which there are no MBO criteria. What happens at the end of the year when the MBO goal is not met but there has been progress on new projects?

There is an enormous body of literature discussing the job of the manager and how to "practice management." Unfortunately, in the real world, executives most often use a process that is simple and superficial: Rather than attempt to determine the quality of the manager's performance, they simply count things. As with downsizing, it's easier than thoughtful analysis.

Principle IV. Evaluating a manager's performance by quantitative measures doesn't necessarily induce behavior in the interest of either the enterprise or the manager.

Benchmarking

A recent trend in evaluating managerial performance is benchmarking, in which similar processes are compared within and across organizations to identify "best practices." A consultant or an internal task force measures specific functions and compares those results to a designated control group. The problem with this approach is that many managers don't operate in an assembly-line, standardized product kind of world, and there can be significant variations in technology and activities from one division to another.

As with MBOs, benchmarks may do more harm than good as the focus shifts from the quality of a transaction to the quantity of transactions completed (or the equivalent cost). For example, once a payables disbursement is authorized, it's unlikely to be further reviewed. Consider, however, a few of the payables reviews that should be performed:

- Completeness/accuracy of accounting codes
- Verification of signature(s) authorizing payment

- Coding to disbursement system
- Determining whether size/nature of disbursement requires special handling
- Diarying payment to appropriate release date
- Determining disbursement mechanism/bank

These are important audits that safeguard the assets of an organization, and any speed-up induced by benchmarks or standards may turn the process into an unchecked assembly line. In some situations the process has turned into a work team competition, where the winning group receives recognition at the end of the month. One consulting client had a pizza party as the weekly prize for the team issuing the most checks! In such situations accuracy is too often sacrificed for speed.

The only appropriate benchmark is the comparison of equivalent things. If you do financial benchmarking, you should select specific functions, cost them, and then ask banks and vendors to bid on those services. For example, you might consider benchmarking the disbursement function. Banks/vendors offer services that accept a file of approved payments and use the preferred payment mechanism. The bank/vendor translates and formats the file and initiates the disbursement.

To develop a benchmark for payables, compare an organization's internal costs to the pricing by a bank/vendor. Then establish alternative scenarios, including:

- Maintaining the current disbursement system (preparing and distributing payments, reconciling bank accounts, and other necessary operations)
- Improving internal processing
  - Analyzing computer requirements to reduce CPU time and computer support
  - Renegotiating banking costs following competitive bidding
  - Reducing space requirements through computer efficiencies and floor redesign

- Outsourcing payment activities to a bank or vendor, including check writing, mailing, reconciling, ACH, EDI, and Fedwire (described in Chapter 5). The bank/vendor verifies the file transmission, registers the issued disbursement, and provides reconciliation and inquiry services.

The benchmark is the price the bank/vendor bids; you must then decide whether the potential savings justify removing this function from your organization's direct control. There are numerous issues to be considered in such a decision, and it should be analyzed by experienced financial managers.

Principle V. Benchmarking may oversimplify a manager's responsibilities, encourage haste in the workplace, and adversely affect product or service quality.

■ CASHFLOW REENGINEERING: THE PRINCIPAL OBJECTIVE

As we've seen, the various systems of defining business and performance objectives are not without flaws. It's important to remember that none of these systems is incorrect, however; in fact, all of them may be correct in different situations and at different times. Customer creation and profitability may sometimes conflict with one another, but they are excellent ideas, and a business cannot long survive without them. Running a business day to day, however, is difficult without a principal objective.

If we define our principal objective as *the continual cashflow reengineering of our organization*, we give the manager and his or her management an ongoing process to guide and evaluate performance. Cash in this context is to be broadly construed, including all sources and uses of the liquidity available to the organization.

Primary liquidity, the cash first called on in a normal business environment, includes operating cashflow, short-term investments, and credit sources. Various techniques of reengineering primary liquidity sources are discussed throughout this book. Secondary liquidity, the cash subject to call in situations of distress, includes renegotiation of contracts and asset liquidation. We obviously reject the tactics of secondary liquidity for cashflow reengineering unless the survival of the organization is severely threatened.

Reengineering is realistic only if it defines a methodology; it is not enough to simply suggest that business processes be redesigned. Managers must have procedures to follow that hopefully don't eliminate much of the workforce. The procedures described in the appendix to this chapter focus on the analysis of cashflow activities and the evaluation of both internal and external alternatives to current processes.

Principle VI. A manager's reengineering plans should be evaluated for their impact both inside and outside the individual business unit. The evaluation should specify problem areas, methods of analysis, and other business units and/or managers with whom cooperation and coordination will be required.

■ ■ ■

CHAPTER 2 APPENDIX

METHODOLOGY FOR ANALYZING AND IMPROVING CASH ACTIVITIES

The analysis and improvement of cashflow activities have become as important as the sale of product for many companies. The methodology described below is useful in documenting cashflow activities and improving an organization's competitiveness and efficiency. It has been used by our consultants in hundreds of studies with clients in the United States and worldwide.

The process of developing a payment stream matrix has been discussed and illustrated in Exhibit 2-2. To prepare a matrix for your organization, list cash and information flows by name, dollar volume, and manager. Selecting significant cash flows (usually those of $1 million or more per month) focuses the effort on those flows most important to the success of the business.

Written procedures and bank reports, along with the cash flow documentation, should be analyzed to identify opportunities for improvement. In developing ideas for improvement, it's important to utilize standard practices and trends, as well as current developments in cash management. Study findings should be presented in a report providing a management summary, recommendations, and cash flow documentation. This may need to be a formal report that explains the methodology and findings to members of management who have not been intimately involved in the study process. The summary should include an evaluation of current cashflow practices in your organization, suggestions for any organizational changes, and a brief review of study findings.

Recommendations should include the following:

- A description of each improvement idea

- A summary of facts supporting the idea

- The potential benefits of the change

- An estimate of implementation costs and hurdles

- A list of open issues that must be resolved prior to implementation. Open issues could include statutory or regulatory issues that need to be clarified by legal counsel, or marketing issues regarding customer reaction to proposed changes.

A Cashflow Flowchart (Exhibit 2-3) and Narrative Description

XYZ COMPANIES
Remittance with Application for Insurance Coverage

Cash and Information Flows

1. The customer submits an application for insurance coverage to an agent representing XYZ. For a new customer, the agent estimates the annual premium and requests a binder check equivalent to 25 percent of the annual premium.

Note: Agents are not required to get a binder check from current XYZ monoline customers who are converting to UP coverage or their customers who currently have coverage through other insurance companies and are transferring coverage to a XYZ policy. Only 60 percent of applications processed by XYZ are accompanied by binder checks.

2. Agents mail the applications and checks to a box number at the central post office (Main Street Post Office) in Anytown. Each SERVICE TEAM has a unique box number, with separate boxes for automotive and homeowners monoline policies.

3. An XYZ mail room employee picks up mail at the post office at 4:00 to 5:00 A.M. daily and again about 6:00 A.M. All mail is opened and sorted in the mail room; one of the sorted batches represents checks with applications. Checks are separated from applications and a duplicate transmittal form is prepared for each check. One copy of the form is attached to the check and one to the application. The check is endorsed for deposit to ABC Bank and stamped with a sequential identification number; the same number is stamped on the application and the transmittal forms. The batch of checks and the batch of applications are taken to the Accounting Unit by 8:00 A.M.

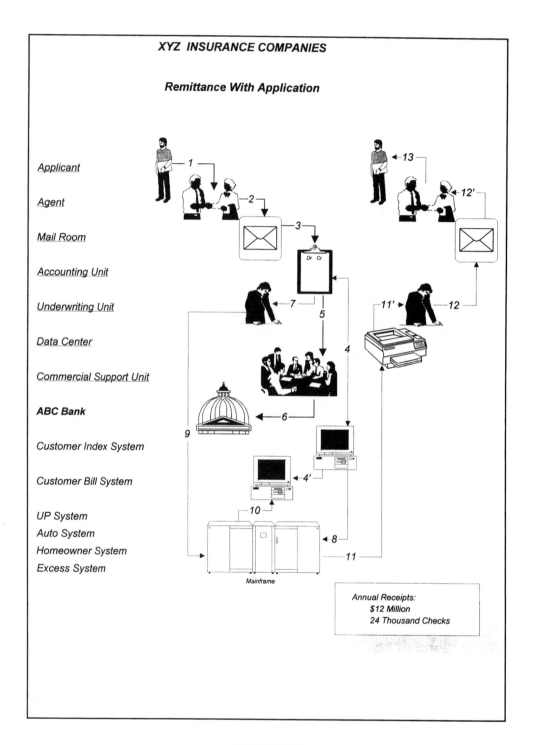

Exhibit 2-3

4. UP applications and checks are given to a general clerk for the SERVICE teams; monoline applications and checks are given the the Customer Index group. Applications are "folderized" and account/policy numbers are assigned through the Customer Index System. The account number is written on the check and transmittal form.

5. Checks are combined into batches of 60 and totalled. The batches are taken to the Commercial Support Unit (1st floor) before 2:00 P.M. daily.

6. The batches of checks are combined with checks from six other units (i.e., Residual Market and five Commercial units), a deposit slip is prepared, the checks are placed in a briefcase and taken to the ABC Bank at Saturn and Pluto Streets for deposit to the XYZ Casualty Co. general account, # 123-4567890, before 3:00 P.M.

7. The applications are sent to the underwriting member of the SERVICE team or Underwriting Unit on the day of receipt. Historically, close to 70 percent of the applications received have been incomplete and have required research, delaying the issuance of a policy. In addition to completing missing information, Underwriting generally orders a motor vehicle report, if the agent did not. A credit report also may be ordered. The process may be completed within ten minutes or may take 30 days or more if an exchange of letters with the applicant is necessary. Although state regulations differ, they frequently mandate completion of the underwriting decision within 60 days from the application date.

8. The Customer Index System runs overnight and sets up new policies in the policy issuance systems: UP System, Auto System, Homeowner System, and/or the Excess System.

9. The underwriting member of the SERVICE team or Underwriting Unit completes the underwriting process and sends the package of information to a data clerk for entry to the appropriate policy issuance system.

10. The policy issuance systems pass files to the Customer Bill System (CBS), which tracks premium and payment history.

11. The policy declaration pages are printed in duplicate at the Data Center the next morning. A scannable (OCR) premium bill also is printed. Various payment options are available, including a 9-payment plan for UP (i.e., 20 percent of premium on first payment, 10 percent on each of next 8 monthly payments), quarterly and annual plan. Quarterly billing is the primary mode of operation; the 9-payment plan is discouraged because of the complexity of adjusting the billing for each policy endorsement during the term. After the initial bill, a $3.00 service charge (soon to be raised to $4.00) is added to each subsequent bill as long as a balance remains outstanding. (Note: Lesser service charges are applied in several states because of state insurance regulations.)

The Underwriting Unit declines 7 to 8 percent of the applications received. A declination notice is produced for these applicants notifying them of the effective date of cancellation of coverage 30 days from the date of the notice. (Note: XYZ is on the risk from the day the agent accepts the application until the effective date of cancellation. A bill for the earned premium during the implied coverage period is sent to the applicant.)

The Data Center delivers the printed output to the SERVICE teams/Underwriting Unit for review and approval.

12. Underwriting releases the policy documents to the Mail Room, where they are inserted into envelopes addressed to the agent, metered, and bundled for mailing. Agent mail is not sent through the presort vendor used for general mailings; these packages are taken to the post office for mailing at the end of the day, about 4:00 P.M.

13. The agent receives the policy information and premium notice, separates and files the copy, and mails or delivers the insured's copy.

chapter

·3·

The Cashflow
Reengineering Process

Vision is the art of seeing things invisible.
—Jonathan Swift (1667–1745)

Whither is fled the *visionary* gleam?
Where is it now, the glory and the dream?
—William Wordsworth (1770–1850)

Our approach to financial reengineering is based on a structured analysis of cashflow alternatives, or "scenarios." This chapter describes the process for specifying and evaluating those scenarios. Before we get into it, however, we need to take a look at a fundamental issue that often confuses the process.

■ MANAGERIAL MYOPIA

Our extensive experience in financial consulting for various national and international organizations has made it clear that the principal areas to benefit from reengineering are those portions of the cashflow timeline that fall outside of traditional financial management. For example, in the portion of the timeline that deals with the receipt of funds, three-fourths of the benefits come from improved methods of issuing invoices and applying cash. In the disbursement portion of the timeline, an equivalent percentage of savings comes from improved invoice and claim review and clearing/funding activity.

The principal reason for this is the assignment of responsibility for cashflow events. In most organizations, cash activities are specifically delegated to finance department staff (such as lockbox, controlled disbursement, and money transfer). These managers, usually with titles such as "assistant treasurer" or "director of financial operations," operate within a well-defined discipline, with access to the expertise of commercial banks, industry groups, and peers. Cashflow activities that precede or follow the treasury function, however, are most often the responsibility of managers with little knowledge about the management of cash. As we discussed in Chapter 2, their focus is on their own problems or goals in the conduct of their businesses (Principle I). For example, invoices may be issued based on marketing or systems convenience; payables may be managed at the convenience of the payables manager.

This "managerial myopia" is also evident in the way most business functions are typically reviewed. A specific product, service, or process will be examined solely within the confines of a specific department or business unit. If the issue is slow processing of mail, for example, the change is usually directed toward the mailroom or the trip to the post office. When bank services are put out to bid, the analysis usually evaluates float, price, customer service, and relationship with the bank/vendor.

The essence of reengineering, however, is to redesign the entire process, not a single step or action within that process. Examination of only one particular element within the cashflow timeline is flawed for the following reasons:

- *The unseen solution.* All possible alternative solutions may not be examined. For example, consider the standard lockbox product. (Note: Various financial terms or products are used in illustrative material throughout this book. Each will be defined as it is used. Definitions are noted with a ➤➤ symbol.)

  ➤➤ A **lockbox** requires that a company directs its customers to send payments to a post office box. That box is monitored by the company's lockbox bank. The bank picks up the mail, brings it back to its processing center, and deposits the items into the company's account. The bank notifies the company of the deposit totals and sends the payment information to them, saving both processing time and internal costs.

  Bidding for lockbox services alone would exclude the possibility that the entire set of collection activities along the cash timeline could be either outsourced or handled internally by the organization. It assumes that those activities are adequately managed and do not have to be examined in a rigorous process.

- *Objective evaluation.* All the elements within each alternative may not be properly examined. For example, the lockbox decision should consider customer service issues and concerns over the company's control of the bank or vendor's processing activities. Both of these issues are difficult to quantify.

- *Timeline element interactions.* The impact of one timeline element on another may not be considered. For example, changing lockbox bank/vendors may impact balances currently available for short-term investments or for compensating concentration banks.

Cash is not the responsibility of any particular functional area, yet it is affected by nearly every operation in an organization. As we noted in the cashflow timeline discussion, activities are tied to cash at each step in the cycle of business activity. For example:

- Salespeople affect cash by the terms they give for down-payments and by the timing of the invoices.

- The credit and collections department affects cash by the way it sets cash discounts, reviews the credit of potential customers, and pursues—or fails to pursue—slow payers.

- Production affects cash by providing adequate inventory to allow the sale to occur.

It should be noted that business activity cycles recur and have a definite (but not identical) pattern of events. For example, an economic cycle has growth, speculation, recession, and recovery, and then begins again. Using this concept, cycles occur for working capital, inventory, and other elements of business activity, which we discuss throughout the book. On the other hand, cashflow reengineering is the understanding of, improvement to, and outsourcing of a cash inflow or outflow, as appropriate. This is not a cyclical event, in that the end of the cashflow does not trigger the beginning of the next flow. A cashflow is a discrete occurrence, although the same cashflow may occur thousands of times in a month, such as cash collection for the sale of your product.

Analyzing these interrelations and reengineering the optimal solution is a difficult process. Because of the difficulty, products and services are usually considered only for specific parts of the problem, and rarely for the entire problem.

Principle VII. Managers tend to focus on only part of a business problem, rather than visualizing the entire problem and all its possible solutions.

■ THE THREE STEPS OF CASHFLOW REENGINEERING

Our approach to reengineering examines the entire cashflow timeline and considers the redesign of all relevant elements. This comprehensive approach consists of three basic steps:

1. Establishing alternative scenarios
2. Quantifing each scenario
3. Creating an "impact table" to compare scenarios

Step One: Establishing Scenarios

The cashflow timeline consists of three basic segments:

1. *Collections*, or the receipt of funds
2. *Concentration*, or the banking and investment of funds
3. *Disbursements*, or the use of funds

A "scenario" is an alternative way of processing one of these segments. There are basically three alternatives:

1. Internal processing
2. Outsourcing
3. A combination of internal processing and outsourcing

With *internal processing* the organization itself performs the timeline activity. For example, internal processing of concentration activities might include managing bank balances, investments, and borrowings, and the development of information for cash forecasting and other purposes.

With *outsourcing* a bank or vendor is hired to handle the timeline activity. Recent corporate initiatives to reduce headcount and internal operating costs have spurred the use of outsourcing. And given the fact that banks and vendors now often use benchmarking, zero error, total quality management (TQM), and other similar programs, there is less concern for outsource service quality. Also, because financial staff has become more involved in various support roles (in sales, for sales financing and/or credit and collections; in systems, for electronic data interchange), there is a greater receptivity to the outsourcing of selected financial activities.

The third and most common approach to processing is *a combination of internal processing and outsourcing.* If an organization used the combination approach for the collection portion of the timeline, it might handle invoicing, cash application, and credit and collection activity, while a bank or vendor handled cash collection and depositing. If the combination approach was used for disbursement activities, the organization might prepare a daily tape of vendor/claim payments (including all remittance advice data, disbursement bank data, and other information) and transmit that tape to a bank or vendor, who would then print and mail the required advices and payments.

Exhibit 3-1 demonstrates nine different scenarios for a large organization with multiple collection sites. A similar approach can be used for other cashflow reengineering reviews, such as those for concentration and disbursement activities. In this example, the "Current System" assumes four sites (A through D) that collect and process receipts. Various pairings or consolidations of these sites are then analyzed, including A and B to B, C and D to D, and all four sites to D. In addition, internal processing improvements and outsourcing through lockboxing are examined.

Step Two: Quantifying the Scenarios

Each segment of the cashflow timeline (collections, concentration, disbursements) involves a number of specific *cost elements.* In order to quantify the scenarios, every cost element in the segment being studied must be determined. In the collection segment, cost elements include the following:

EXHIBIT 3-1   Alternative Scenarios for the Collection Timeline

Multiple Sites

Each of four sites (labeled A–D) continues to collect and process its current mix of business.

Paired Site Consolidation

Receipt processing at two sites, with the most expensive check processing costs consolidated into the least expensive sites.

Equipment:	3 reader-sorters (25% reduction) and one MICR encoder in consolidated operations
Labor:	25% reduction (based upon discussions with site management)
Overhead:	Projected rates for sites based upon current incremental lease rates
Banking costs:	Availability float (in days) basically unchanged from current site experience; courier charges unchanged (not dependent on volume); service fee per item charge roughly 10% less than current all-in per item price (based on increased volumes)

Fully Consolidated

All receipt processing from all sites is consolidated into the least expensive site.

Equipment:	50% reduction to 4 reader-sorters and 2 MICR encoders
Labor:	50% reduction
Overhead:	Projected rates for sites based upon current incremental lease rates

---

EXHIBIT 3-1   Continued

Banking costs: Availability float (days) taken from float model calculation across all four sites combined; courier charges unchanged (not dependent on volume); service fee per item roughly 20% less than current all-in per item price (based on increased volumes)

       Volume: Sum of two combined sites

Improve Internal

Pick up mail as soon as available from post office; add a second midday/early afternoon deposit to make all afternoon/evening deposit cutoffs currently missed; renegotiate bank fees; charge clients for returns/redeposits to recoup related bank fees; liberalize rules to expedite processing of exceptions.

Equipment: No impact

       Labor: 10% increase in collections full-time equivalents (FTEs) to support parallel and/or second-shift processing that will prioritize receipts and meet two deposit deadlines daily

Overhead: No impact on rate

Banking costs: Availability float (days) taken from float model calculations (based on meeting key afternoon/evening availability cutoff times); courier charges increased by $125/month for a second deposit pickup (assumes second deposit run can be accomplished within an existing courier route—otherwise costs $25/day)

      Volumes: Slight decline in volume due to elimination of some exception processing

                                Continued

EXHIBIT 3-1 Continued

Outsource/0% or 50%

Outsource to a lockbox, with the bank/vendor intercepting the mail directly from the post office, processing all nonexception receipts, depositing as processed, returning all exceptions by daily courier, and providing a daily transmission of all accounts receivable data (captured from optically scanning the receipt coupon scanline).

Equipment:	None needed
Labor:	Eliminate all collection FTEs plus 20% of management; all exception processing FTEs remain to handle exception items
Overhead:	No impact
Banking costs:	Availability float as measured by float model; courier charges assumed to be similar to those currently experienced; per item prices are based upon a survey of bank/vendor lockbox service providers
Volume:	Same as under Improve Internal scenarios
Total per item:	Same calculations as under Improve Internal scenarios

Equipment

- Mail openers to mechanically slice and extract documents from envelopes
- MICR encoders to encode the amount of the written check to the right of the preprinted MICR line

» The **MICR** (magnetic ink character recognition) line is printed on the bottom of checks and remittance documents in a special character set that can be read by optical scanners. Normally, such data includes bank account addresses, check numbers, and account data.

- Reader-sorters to read and sort checks based on MICR line data, prepare bank deposit tickets, and create a file to update accounts receivable

Labor

- Collections labor to process remittance data and operate the equipment used for remittance processing
- Exceptions labor to process nonstandard payments, including changes of address, mismatches of the check and billed amount, inquiries, disputes, or requests for additional time to pay
- Management to supervise all collection activities

Overhead

- Rent (as allocated to the space utilized by the collections area)
- Utilities (as allocated to the collections area)

Banking Costs

- *Availability float*—the time required for the local bank to collect checks deposited— translated to cost per item
- Courier costs to transport checks to the bank for depositing
- Bank fees to compensate the bank for various services provided

Equipment, labor, and overhead costs are derived from budgets or from the record of expenses reported in the general ledger. Banking costs are not easily derived from either source; they require careful review of the bank's invoice, called an *account analysis*.

➻ The **account analysis** is the invoice a bank provides
to its corporate customers. This document lists balance data and fees charged for specific services. (For
a complete description, see the Chapter 3 Appendix).

Exhibit 3-2   Collection Processing, A–D Site Costs

Equipment				
Mail Opener				
Depreciation	$0		$0	
(Includes Maintenance)				
Reader/Sorter				
Lease	$2,000		$2,000	
Maintenance	$1,000		$1,000	
MICR Encoder				
Depreciation	$0		$0	
Maintenance	$70		$70	
Subtotal	$3,070		$3,070	
Labor:				
Collections	5.50	FTE	7.50	FTE
Exceptions	5.00	FTE	10.50	FTE
Other	0.10	FTE	0.10	FTE
Management	0.25	MGR	0.25	MGR
Subtotal (FTEs)	10.60	FTE	18.10	FTE
Subtotal	$16,960		$28,960	
Overhead:				
Rent: (Includes Utilities)				
Per Employee	40 X $10/SF		40 x $22/SF	
Subtotal	$353		$1,327	
Banking Costs:				
Availability Float (Days)	1.55		1.23	
Availability Float	$9,667		$12,725	
Courier Charges	$513		$500	
Service Fees	$11,238	($.111)	$6,211	($.055)
Subtotal	$21,418		$19,436	
Total Costs	$41,801		$52,793	
Item Volume	71,400		78,820	
Total Per Item	$0.585		$0.670	

Continuing with the example shown in Exhibit 3-1, Exhibit 3-2 provides costs at each site, A through D. Exhibit 3-3 shows costs for Site A with various internal improvement and outsourcing combinations. Exhibit 3-4 includes the same data

$0		$0		$0	
$2,000		$2,000		$8,000	
$1,000		$1,000		$4,000	
$0		$0		$0	
$70		$70		$280	
$3,070		$3,070		$12,280	
6.00	FTE	4.00	FTE	23.00	FET
5.00	FTE	5.50	FTE	26.00	FTE
0.10	FTE	0.10	FTE	0.40	FTE
0.25	MRG	0.25	MRG	1.00	MRG
11.10	FTE	9.60	FTE	49.40	FTE
$17,760		$15,360		$79,040	
40 x $11/SF		40 x $12/SF			
$407		$384		$2,472	
1.94		1.85			
$13,898		$10,103		$46,393	
$680		$500		$2,193	
$9,055	($.083)	$6,312	($.095)	$32,816	($.084)
$23,633		$16,915		$81,402	
$44,870		$35,729		$175,194	
76,720		46,620		273,560	
$0.585		$0.766		$0.640	

EXHIBIT 3-3   Collection Processing, Site A Options

Monthly Cost Categories	Current		Site A Internal Processing Improvements 10%	
Equipment				
Mail Opener	$0		$0	
Reader/Sorter	$3,000		$3,000	
MICR Encoder	$70		$70	
Subtotal	$3,070		$3,070	
Labor:				
Collections	5.50	FTE	6.05	FTE
Exceptions	5.00	FTE	5.00	FTE
Other	0.10	FTE	0.10	FTE
Management	0.25	MGR	0.25	MGR
Subtotal	10.60	FTE	11.15	FTE
Subtotal	$16,960		$17,840	
Overhead:				
Per Employee	40 X $10/SF		40 x $10/SF	
Subtotal	$353		$372	
Banking Costs:				
Avail. Float (Days)	1.55		1.33	
Availability Float	$9,667		$8,295	
Courier Charges	$513		$638	
Service Fees	$11,238	($.111)	$8,160	($.08)
Subtotal	$21,418		$17,093	
Total Costs:	$41,801		$38,375	
Item Volume	71,400		71,400	
Total Per Item	$0.585		$0.537	

NOTE: As calculations for Sites B, C, and D are similar, spreadsheets for these cases have been deleted from Exhibit 3–3.

				Outsource			
25%		50%		50%		100%	
$0		$0		$0		$0	
$3,000		$3,000		$0		$0	
$70		$70		$0		$0	
$3,070		$3,070		$0		$0	
5.89	FTE	5.23	FTE	0.00	FTE	0.00	FTE
4.85	FTE	4.25	FTE	5.00	FTE	4.25	FTE
0.10	FTE	0.08	FTE	0.10	FTE	0.08	FTE
0.24	MGR	0.21	MGR	0.19	MGR	0.17	MGR
10.84	FTE	9.56	FTE	5.10	FTE	4.33	FTE
$17,344		$15,296		$8,160		$6,928	
40 x $10/SF		40 x $10/SF		40 x $10/SF		40 x $10/SF	
$361		$319		$170		$144	
1.33		1.33		1.33		1.33	
$7,830		$5,972		$8,295		$5,972	
$638		$638		$513		$513	
$7,703	($.08)	$5,875	($.08)	$17,340	($.17)	$12,485	($.17)
$16,171		$12,485		$26,148		$18,970	
$36,946		$31,170		$34,478		$26,042	
68,500		63,500		71,400		66,000	
$0.539		$0.491		$0.483		$0.395	

EXHIBIT 3-4   Collection Processing, Consolidation to B

Monthly Cost Categories	Current Sites A&B Combined		Consolidate To Site B	
Equipment				
Mail Opener	$0		$0	
Reader/Sorter	$6,000		$4,500	
MICR Encoder	$$140		$70	
Subtotal	$6,140		$4,570	
Labor:				
Collections	10.00	FTE	7.50	FTE
Exceptions	10.50	FTE	7.88	FTE
Other	0.20	FTE	0.15	FTE
Management	0.50	MGR	0.33	MGR
Subtotal (FTEs)	21.20	FTE	15.86	FTE
Subtotal	$33,920		$25,376	
Overhead: (Rent & Utilities)				
Per Employee	40 X $11/SF		40 x $11/SF	
Subtotal	$777.33		$581.53	
Banking Costs:				
Availability Float (Days)			1.94	
Availability Float	$24,001		$24,493	
Courier Charges	$1,180		$680	
Service Fees	$15,367	($.087)	$13,215	($.075)
Subtotal	$40,548		$38,390	
Total Costs:	$81,385		$68,917	
Item Volume	176,200		176,200	
Total Per Item	$0.462		$0.391	

NOTE: As calculations for the consolidation of Sites C and D to D, and for Sites A through D to D are similar, spreadsheets have been deleted from Exhibit 3-4.

Improve Internal		Outsource (Lockbox)	
0%	**50%**	**50%**	**100%**
$0	$0	$0	$0
$4,500	$4,500	$0	$0
$70	$70	$0	$0
$4,570	$4,570	$0	$0
20.00 FTE	13.70 FTE	0.00 FTE	0.00 FTE
21.00 FTE	13.40 FTE	6.70 FTE	7.88 FTE
0.40 FTE	0.26 FTE	0.15 FTE	0.15 FTE
1.00 MGR	0.56 MGR	0.22 MGR	0.26 MGR
42.40 FTE	27.92 FTE	7.07 FTE	8.29 FTE
$67,840	$44,672	$11,312	$13,264
40 x $11/SF	40 x $11/SF	40 x $11/SF	40 x $11/SF
$1,554.67	$1,023.73	$259.23	$303.97
1.41	1.41	1.42	1.42
$17,802	$12,817	$18,561	$21,867
$2,000	$2,000	$1,200	$1,200
$11,453 ($.065)	$8,246 ($.065)	$28,191 ($.19)	$51,976 ($.19)
$31,256	$23,064	$47,953	$75,044
$105,221	$73,330	$59,525	$88,612
176,200	126,864	148,375	273,560
$0.597	$0.578	$0.401	$0.324

as Exhibit 3-3 for the pairing of A and B to B. (Calculations for sites B, C, and D, for the pairing of C and D to D, and for the combination of the four sites to D are similar to those in Exhibits 3-3 and 3-4 and have been deleted in the interest of simplicity.)

Step Three: Creating a Scenario Impact Table

The amount of data developed in the previous step can be overwhelming. A summary of the results, the *scenario impact table*, helps organize the critical summary data for easier review and analysis.

Normally there will be several components to the table; in our lockbox illustration (see Exhibit 3-5), the vertical axis contains the alternative scenarios and the horizontal axis contains the site combinations. You can develop additional scenarios by visualizing different combinations from the table. In Exhibit 3-5, for example, regular collection receipts could be lockboxed, with exceptions processed at the sites, at pairs of sites, or at a single designated site, creating several additional scenarios.

The first scenario in the table shows the current system of the four sites; those that follow add the changes listed in Exhibit 3-1. There are ten live "cases" presented in shaded boxes, one each for scenarios 1 through 8 and two for scenario 9. (In scenario 9 sites A and B are consolidated to B, sites C and D to D, and all four sites are consolidated to to site B). Any number of additional scenarios could be developed, as we have noted. Of the ten cases, perhaps three are attractive from a cost perspective: scenario 6, which deals with lockboxing, and scenario 9, which involves two approaches to site consolidation. (Scenarios 7 and 8 wouldn't normally be considered, as the additional lockboxes cause the cost per item to increase slightly due to the loss of quantity pricing and other costs.)

Why do so many organizations choose not to conduct this thorough an analysis? It may be they're simply avoiding the complexities and going for the easy solution. After all, our examination of collection activity scenarios involves the costs of five organizational units:

No.	Scenarios	Site A	Site B	Site C	Site D	Total Co.
	EXHIBIT 3-5 Scenario Impact Table					
1	Current system: No change	58.5¢	67.0¢	58.5¢	76.6¢	^ 64.0¢
2	Current system: 10% internal improvements	53.7¢	* 70.0¢	* 55.9¢	* 70.4¢	^ 62.3¢
3	Current system: 25% internal improvements	53.9¢	* 68.7¢	* 56.6¢	* 69.1¢	^ 62.0¢
4	Current system: 50% internal improvements	49.1¢	* 66.5¢	* 55.1¢	* 67.2¢	^ 61.5¢
5	Outsource half to 1 bank/vendor lockbox; keep half internal	NA	NA	NA	NA	40.1¢
6	Outsource all to 1 bank/vendor lockbox	NA	NA	NA	NA	32.4¢
7	Outsource all to 2 banks/vendor lockboxes	NA	NA	NA	NA	* 41.0¢
8	Outsource all to 3 banks/vendor lockboxes	NA	NA	NA	NA	* 42.5¢
9	Consolidate sites A-B to B & sites C-D to D; sites A-D to B	NA	39.1¢	NA	* 43.7¢	* 37.2¢

Notes: Lockbox costs are estimated prior to formal request-for-proposal.
Shaded boxes are "live" cases.
*   Spreadsheet not included in Chapter 3 appendix
^   Not a live "case"; shown only for reference
NA =   Scenario not applicable for that case

1. Mailroom operations to receive, open, and distribute mail.

2. Accounting to process incoming receipts and to apply cash to open receivables.

3. Treasury to prepare the deposit ticket and to manage cash in banks.

4. Information Systems to manage data flows.

5. Customer Service to handle inquiries and other matters.

With all the various functions and cost elements involved, the correct course of action is more difficult to determine than if only a single function or cost is being examined. Consequently, many organizations choose the relatively easy course: They do nothing, or they make a decision (often to downsize) without considering all the relevant issues.

> **Principle VIII.** Managers tend to focus on either improving current systems or on outsourcing; the best reengineering efforts generally utilize combinations of *both* throughout a collection, concentration, or disbursement process.

■ QUALITY ISSUES

We've found that financial decisions are all too often primarily quantitative: Managers simply select the lowest-cost option. In addition to cost and time, however, reengineering involves service and other nonquantifiable issues. In our example, the three low-cost cases should certainly be evaluated in tandem with relevant service issues. This evaluation might include the following questions:

If Sites Are Consolidated

- *Sunk or avoidable costs.* Are costs avoidable or sunk at each site (leases, capital equipment, maintenance contracts)? This is one of the most difficult questions to answer in analyzing costs. For example, a printer purchased four years ago has a useful life of six more years, seven before it is fully depreciated. If there are no alternative uses for that printer, the undepreciated cost must be added to the price bid by the bank or vendor, or the printer must be sold with an appropriate accounting adjustment.

- *Severance costs.* What are the costs of terminating employees (severance, job search assistance, loss of experienced personnel)? Organizations have discovered that employee termination costs can be significant, particularly when there's a core of long-term employees. It's not unusual for employee termination costs due to reengineering to average more than 25 percent of annual labor costs. Many affected workers are often reassigned to other positions, however, reducing the net loss.

- *Service quality.* Are there concerns for service quality? Are there unique processes that would be disrupted? Are customers accustomed to dealing with certain service personnel? Customer service issues should be carefully examined to determine whether the vendor can duplicate the support provided by employees of the organization. Exhibit 3-6 lists customer service issues.

If Lockboxing Is Implemented

- *Error rates.* What is the bank/vendor's error rate in processing collection items? (For example, does the bank/vendor calculate processing error rates per 10,000 transactions?) In recent years, banks and other vendors have become aware of the need for proof of quality; they have developed methods to count errors and determine their causes and to chart error trends over time.

- *Timing of information transmittal.* Are the deposit reporting and data transmission times early enough to meet the organization's financial and systems requirements? Does the balance report occur early enough so that treasury activities can be completed on time? Is data transmission at a time acceptable to systems? Any bank or vendor service will interface on a frequent basis (hourly, daily) with appropriate functions within the business. Treasury will require data on bank deposits and investments; receivables will need information on invoices paid. All of this will have to be at the convenience of systems so that

---

EXHIBIT 3-6   Customer Service Issues

- **_Customer service representatives._** Does the bank or vendor have dedicated service representatives (reps)? Is there a pool of service personnel or are specific individuals assigned to the account? Many companies prefer a team partnership with a primary and secondary rep available through direct telephone access. Regardless of the organization of the reps, is there a demonstrated commitment to resolve inquiries within the current or the next business day? Does the bank or vendor provide an implementation team to establish new products and services? Are the various reps provided frequent training on products and on customer communication skills? Are the hours of contact access reflective of U.S. (or global) hours of operation (ten or twelve hours of coverage)?

- **_Automated inquiry._** Many situations don't require customer-rep interaction, and can be quickly resolved through automated access to bank/vendor databases. Is such access provided through a single-system platform in a unified PC workstation? Is there an automated tracking system to monitor progress on inquiries?

---

transmissions can be received and processed without problems or delays.

- _Disaster recovery._ Does the bank/vendor have an adequate disaster recovery process? (Is there a dedicated bank/vendor owned off-site location? Is there coverage through another bank or vendor?) Exhibit 3-7 presents a listing of disaster recovery issues.

In addition to addressing these quality concerns, the low-cost cases should also be weighed against the current situation of multiple collection sites (scenario 1). Decisions need to be made regarding the cost of retaining the status quo as compared to the most viable alternatives. Any decision to reengineer must consider whether saving "X"¢ per item is worth the uncertainty of consolidation or outsourcing. Cashflow scenario analysis can assist you in reaching that decision.

EXHIBIT 3-7   Disaster Recovery Issues

- ■ *Disaster experience/simulations.* Disaster experience may include actual experience, such as the World Trade Center bombing (February 1993), Hurricane Andrew (August 1992), and the Chicago flood (April 1992); and/or it may involve periodic testing. The bank or vendor should comment on lessons learned during actual situations and should explain the protocols used in simulations. For example, in a test, was data recreated by the opening of the next business day? How often are these drills conducted?

- ■ *Organization.* The bank or vendor should have a dedicated disaster recovery or contingency planning manager who reports to a steering committee or a senior executive. Responsibilities should include the preparation and coordination of a comprehensive plan describing precise actions necessary in any disaster situation, particularly for critical areas (money transfer, check processing, and trade settlement). Such plans must be consistent with the rules and guidelines of all governing bodies (Office of the Comptroller of the Currency, Federal Deposit Insurance Corporation, etc.).

- ■ *Technology backup.* Technology redundancy should include the following:
  - A sophisticated communication network with comprehensive recovery capabilities
  - Automatic hardware, software, and telecommunications switching
  - Power backup including dual power feeds, auxiliary power systems, and generators
  - Integrated backup recovery site capabilities either at a parallel site or through an independent provider
  - Redundancy throughout the critical operating environment to eliminate single failure points

> **Principle IX.** Managers who focus only on the *quantitative* measurement of alternative courses of action often fail to recognize essential *qualitative* factors.

In summary, cashflow scenarios all involve either some improvement in internal processing or the use of outsourcing. Not every activity can or should be seriously considered for outsourcing; in fact, many functions are not available from banks or vendors except at an unrealistically high price or with serious concerns for quality. Exhibit 3-8 shows internal processing and outsourcing of financial functions in the typical business practice.

Although new outsourcing services are constantly being developed, some functions will probably always remain internally processed. The manager's job is to continually explore all

EXHIBIT 3-8 Cash, Internal Processing, and Outsourcing Opportunities

Typical Business Practice	Collection Timeline	Concentration and Banking	Disbursement Timeline
Internal processing	Cash application to accounts receivable	Cash forecasting	Review/approval of vendor payments
Traditionally outsourced	Lockbox	Repetitive money transfer	Reconciliation of bank accounts
New outsource service (developed in the past two years and offered by banks or vendors)	Imaging of remittance documents	Foreign exchange real-time money transfer	Comprehensive payment product

possibilities to make certain that his organization operates as efficiently as possible. That's the crux of good management.

Principle X. The essence of management is the continual exploration of opportunities to improve the performance of the organization. The manager must constantly review activities by competitors and product/service offerings by banks and vendors and be prepared to change his or her business procedures to accommodate new technology and new methods.

■ THE VISION THING

A major concept in the reengineering literature is *vision*, the idea that a successful organization must continually redefine its customers, markets, and products. A new vision may involve dismantling and rebuilding the infrastructure of the organization to meet newly defined business requirements. Having a vision for an organization is not a new idea; the outstanding statement on the subject of defining a market—made by Theodore Levitt in 1960—was one of its earliest expressions ("Marketing Myopia," *Harvard Business Review*, Vol. 38, July-August 1960, pp. 45–56). Levitt's "vision" of marketing shifted focus from the sale of the product to the needs of the customer.

Over the years, business experts have complained that a company cannot succeed without a vision, and many have written books about how to go about "getting it." No book can tell you what your business should become, however; that is something that should be continually reexamined by the CEO and his or her staff. And given the accessibility of market and product intelligence and the profusion of strategy consultants and planners, arriving at a vision is hardly the most challenging problem most organizations face.

What is the most challenging management problem? Deciding on the most effective and efficient course of action to attain your vision. The premise of this book is that management must use a logical and thorough process to examine all reasonable courses of action (scenarios) in order to select the best of those actions. Properly structured procedures—based on quantitative *and* qualitative factors—will lead to the correct decision. This process should not result in cataclysmic changes to the organization—to the managers and workers—*unless* all other reengineering possibilities have been examined and all reasonable changes attempted.

■ ■ ■

CHAPTER 3 APPENDIX

THE ACCOUNT ANALYSIS

The account analysis is the monthly invoice many banks provide to their corporate customers. Although there is no universal format, the illustration below provides data in a typical layout used by banks.

Sample Account Analysis			
Average ledger balance			$575,276
Less: average float			520,433
Average collected balance			54,843
Less: reserve requirement	At 10.00%		5,484
Average earning balance			49,359
Earnings credit rate (ECR)	At 2.75%		$113.11
Charge for Services	**Quantity**	**Unit Price**	**Service Charge**
FDIC charge			$25.00
Account maintenance			15.00
Deposits-unencoded	77	.15	11.55
Deposits-encoded-this fed	345	.115	39.68
Deposits-encoded-other feds	674	.13	87.62
Returned items	56	3.00	168.00
Checks paid	550	.15	82.50
Paid items-ACH	105	.135	14.18
Total charge for services			$443.53
Net due for services			$330.42

Average ledger balance The average daily amount in the bank account, calculated from each prior night's balance plus credits (such as deposits) less debits (such as checks clearing against the account).

Average float The average daily amount of these funds, including funds in the process of being collected all the way through to checks in the process of clearing through the banking system. As we'll see in Chapter 6, all checks deposited must clear back to the bank on which they were drawn ("the drawee bank") before credit for those checks is granted to the depositor. This process normally takes up to two business days for checks written on U.S. banks.

Average collected balance The difference between average balance and average float, representing funds that may be used, spent, or withdrawn from the bank by the depositor.

Reserve requirement An amount established by the Federal Reserve to support the liquidity of the banking system. The required reserve is an amount that cannot be lent by the bank to borrowers; it is set aside in the form of currency or deposits at the Federal Reserve. No ECR credit (see below) is earned by reserve requirement amounts.

Average earning balance The amount on which a credit is earned by the corporate depositor. Banks are prohibited by Federal Reserve Regulation Q (12 C.F.R. Part 17) from paying interest on checking account (demand deposit) balances. Intense competition for depositors during the Great Depression led to high interest rates that could not be supported by lending income, leading to the failure of numerous banks. As a result, Congress passed legislation (the Banking Act of 1933) prohibiting the payment of interest on demand deposits.

Earnings credit rate (ECR) An interest allowance against the cost of bank services. Commercial banks are prohibited from paying interest on balances in corporate demand deposit accounts (DDAs) by the Federal Reserve's Regulation Q. To compensate corporations for DDA balances, banks developed the ECR, a noninterest credit used to pay for charges accrued for services rendered. It is usually pegged to the 91-day U.S. Treasury Bill rate, or to a mix of various overnight money market rates.

FDIC charge A mandatory insurance charge imposed by the Federal Deposit Insurance Corporation to maintain a fund to pay depositors of failed banks.

Account maintenance A basic charge to cover overhead costs associated with services provided by the bank for accounts.

The following charges represent selected services that this particular bank provides to its corporate depositors; it is certainly not intended to represent a comprehensive listing of bank services. The quantity, per item charge, and total monthly charge are indicated for each listed service.

Deposits Checks presented for credit to the account. *Unencoded* checks are presented as received from the depositor's customers; *encoded* checks have been MICR-encoded in the lower right corner with the check amount, using special MICR printing equipment. *This fed* are checks drawn on a bank in the same Federal Reserve District as the bank in which they are deposited. *Other fed* items are checks drawn on banks outside of the depository banks; they are slightly more expensive to clear. There are twelve Federal Reserve Districts in the United States.

Returned items Checks deposited that were not honored by the drawee bank. These are usually due to insufficient funds ("NSF") in the maker's account, but may also result from the maker stopping payment on the check. There is a charge for the handling of returned items.

Checks paid Checks written against the account by the corporation and honored by the bank.

Paid items-EFT Electronic payments through the ACH; see Chapter 5.

Net due for services The net of total charge for services less the earnings credit allowance.

chapter

·4·

The Outsourcing Alternative

*By **magic numbers** and persuasive sound.*
—William Congreve (1670 –1729)

The Walrus and the Carpenter
Were walking close at hand:
They wept like anything to see
*Such **quantities** of sand:*
"If this were only cleared away,"
They said, "it would be grand!"

"If seven maids with seven mops
Swept it for half a year,

Do you suppose," the Walrus said,
"That they could get it clear?"
"I doubt it," said the Carpenter,
And shed a bitter tear.

—Lewis Carroll (1832–1898)

As we've seen, reengineering consists of three basic scenarios used alone or in combination: retaining the current system, improving the current system, and outsourcing. This chapter discusses a logical and objective approach to outsourcing. Chapter 5 evaluates product planning, pricing, and profitability analysis. Chapters 6 through 9 review opportunities to improve your current system.

■ SELECTING A BANK OR VENDOR

Throughout this book we'll be talking about banks and the relationship between banks and corporations because of the obvious role they play in receiving deposits, holding and investing funds, and supporting disbursement activities. We'll also be looking at financial service companies, many of which offer certain nonbanking services for cashflow reengineering, such as accounts receivable and payable products. Some financial service companies can also provide bank access, but only banks can be members of the Federal Reserve System and have access to the various clearing systems.

Organizations do business with banks and vendors for a variety of reasons. Some of them are quite logical:

- Participation in credit
- Quality services
- Location
- Product technology
- Survivor in possible merger

Often, however, outsourcing has more to do with an unstated "special connection" between organizations and their banks or vendors, especially those in a long-time relationship:

- Senior management a shareholder and/or on the board of directors

- Logistical difficulties in changing bank or vendor

- Personal relationships with bank/vendor personnel

These "reasons"—though not entirely objective—are based on realistic concerns; others are highly questionable and should clearly be reexamined in the current business environment:

- "Been with this bank/vendor for 75 years"

- "Marketing demands local bank accounts for relationship reasons"

- "Terrific food in the bank's dining room"

An organization's relationship with a bank usually transcends objective analysis—it's often little more than a feeling or attitude. It might relate to the time years ago when the bank continued to support the business through a difficult period, or when a vendor worked all weekend to fix a systems problem or to complete a filing for a stock underwriting. These special connections are difficult to refute, yet hard to quantify when bidding services out to the "best" provider.

Purchase of financial services (other than advisory or consulting services) is not unlike the purchase of any product in which features and pricing may vary significantly by vendor. Organizations typically use a semiformal approach when deciding to outsource. They make a request, either in person or by letter, for information on specific products. This approach has a number of weaknesses, two of which are:

1. Banks or vendors in the existing relationship tend to receive preferential treatment; in many cases, vendors providing excellent products are not even invited to bid.

2. The focus is on a few product features, or on price, at the exclusion of other attributes that may in fact be more important to the overall goals of the organization.

To counteract these weaknesses, two critical steps should be taken in any outsourcing decision: the RFI and the RFP.

The RFI

The RFI, or request-for-information, is a formal information-gathering effort. It is preceded by a more informal process of gathering information from a wide array of sources, including:

Publications:	Articles and directories in financial journals Subscription or free distribution newsletters (such as *Leahy Newsletter* or *Treasury Views*)
Referrals:	Professional association contacts, accountants, attorneys, personal contacts
Sales calls:	Banker/vendor calls, visits to exhibitor booths at conferences

It is important that organizations maintain a continuous effort to explore the marketplace for new product ideas and capabilities. This ongoing, informal process will help develop a file of banks and vendors able to bid on specific services.

The RFI is the first step to be taken once a decision is made to solicit formal bids. This document, usually one to two pages in length, queries banks and vendors on experience, technological capabilities, creditworthiness, and interest in preparing a formal proposal. Exhibit 4-1 shows a typical RFI letter.

In our experience about one-quarter of the banks and vendors who are sent RFIs will decline to bid, usually because they don't offer the service or are unable meet minimum technical requirements. An organization should therefore send out about a dozen RFI letters and expect that the final list of candidate bidders will include about eight names.

The RFP

The RFP, or request-for-proposal, is a formal document soliciting responses to specific questions about the vendor's product or service. The RFP begins with a description of your organization, including its locations, number of transactions, banks and vendors currently used, and other pertinent data. It may

EXHIBIT 4-1   RFI Letter

Dear [name]:

We are in the process of considering banks or non-bank vendors for [describe services]. Our company is [describe company and its business]. The purpose of this letter is to solicit a statement of interest in answering a request-for-proposal (RPF) to be issued on or about [date]. The [service] must be fully operational by [future date].

The initial volume is approximately [number] items per month, with volume expected to grow to [future number] items within 2-3 years. We require that the bank/vendor provide the following operations: [describe].

Please indicate your responses to the attached questionnaire and return the completed information by [date] to [address].

- Do you provide the specified service? If so, how long have you been in the business? What are the sites where the service is provided?

- How long will it take to begin service if you're the selected service provider?

- What data capture (or other) technologies do you use?

- What data transmission protocols do you support?

- What is the credit rating of your organization?

- Are you interested in bidding for this business? If so, who is the appropriate contact person?

Please contact me with any questions regarding this request-for-information. We must have your response by [date].

(Close)

then state the specific requirements of the RFP, including the timing of the selection process and of product implementation.

The following exhibits (4-2 to 4-6) illustrate the type of concerns that might be included in a lockbox RFP. A comprehensive set of materials involved in a retail lockbox RFP review are included as Book Appendices A–D.

Exhibit 4-2: Basic description of the bidder.

Exhibit 4-3: General qualifications of the bidder, to determine basic competence and capabilities.

Exhibit 4-4: Product data, to determine the mechanics of processing for the product or service.

Exhibit 4-5: Buyer's processing requirements, the "musts" and "wants" of the buyer.

Exhibit 4-6: Certification of service capability, usually presented as a multiple choice document of essential service elements. The bidder is required to affix his or her initials to blanks for the answers "Yes," "No," or "Partial." Any "Partial" response should be explained. The certification is then signed by the authorized representative of the bank or vendor as a form of contract to hold bidders responsible for statements made in the proposal.

Exhibit 4-7: Supplemental information, to clarify and explain statements in the proposal.

EXHIBIT 4-2   Bidder Description

Briefly describe your organization, including lines of business, total assets, ratings, and organizational structure. Include your annual report. Describe your client team, including all individuals likely to be assigned should bid business be awarded.

Does your organization have a particular commitment to the widget industry? Provide a listing of current clients, including types of activities provided and length of relationship. If you are a bank, discuss your position on the allocation of credit to customers.

EXHIBIT 4-3 General Qualifications of the Bidder

1. Monthly volume in total and for largest three customers

2. General workflow description

3. Equipment used in processing

4. Problem resolution procedures

5. Bank/vendor output records for receivables/payables accounting

6. Methods and timing of data transmission

7. Mechanisms for funds transfer

8. Timing of balance report on daily activity

EXHIBIT 4-4 Product Specific Issues *(Assumes Lockbox)*

1. Flow of mail through bidder's postal facility

2. Zipcode arrangements (unique, zip + 4, other)

3. Schedule of daily and weekend post office collections

4. Delivery site and resulting delay of mail distribution on bidder's premises

5. Staffing and experience of lockbox operation

6. Maximum daily volumes that can be processed for same-day ledger credit

7. Timing/security of transmission of lockbox data, including remittance media

8. Error rate in lockbox processing

EXHIBIT 4-5   Buyer's Processing Requirements
(Assumes Lockbox)

---

1. Specific volume projections, now and in three years, at peak and average

2. Geographic distribution of customers

3. Processing exceptions as to payee, check date, non-matching dollar amounts, missing check signature, and foreign items

4. Handling of customer correspondence

5. Anticipated data capture requirements from scanline or from remittance documents

6. Procedures for charging for NSF items

7. Delivery procedures for remittance advices, deposit slips, and other materials

8. Data transmission baud rates, timing, and security

Exhibit 4-8: Pricing analysis, including data from the bank or vendor on the following:

- Period of price guarantee
- Formula used to convert service charges to balance equivalents (for banks)
- Derivation of earnings credit rate (ECR) (for banks)
- A pro forma pricing analysis based on all relevant charges to provide service.

   A pro forma analysis describes each element of the service, the projected pricing per element (in fees and balances at the assumed volumes), and the total monthly cost of the product. If the bidder is a bank, pricing will be provided in a monthly account analysis, as described in Chapter 3. The pro forma is important because actual price depends on numerous variables and the final actual cost may be hidden in the complexity of the proposal language.

EXHIBIT 4-6   Certification of Service Capability

Please complete this section, indicating to what extent the lockbox can meet each of the service requests. Explain all "Partial" answers.

A. Lockbox volumes

Yes ____No ____Partial ____

B. Same-day ledger credit for all items

Received

Yes ____No ____Partial ____

C. Lockbox processing procedures

1. Processing of checks

Yes ____No ____Partial ____

2. Data capture from remittances

Yes ____No ____Partial ____

D. Return items

Yes ____No ____Partial ____

E. Data transmission for cash

application

Yes ____No ____Partial ____

etc.

EXHIBIT 4-7   Supplemental Information

---

1. Product brochures

2. Sample contract or agreement of service

3. Postal survey data on mail and availability times (assumes lockbox)

4. Sample output from bank or vendor processing

5. Customer references

6. Complete product pricing schedule

7. Chart of service area organization

8. Implementation checklist

EXHIBIT 4-8   Pro Forma Pricing Analysis

		Bank A		Bank B		Bank C	
	Quantity	Unit Price	Service Charge	Unit Price	Service Charge	Unit Price	Service Charge
Account maintenance	1		$ 40.00		$ 50.00		$ 75.00
Deposits-unencoded	77	$0.150	11.55	$0.130	10.00	$0.125	9.60
Deposits-encoded-this fed	345	$0.115	39.68	$0.135	46.60	$0.130	44.85
Deposits-encoded-other feds	674	$0.130	87.62	$0.150	101.10	$0.140	94.35
Returned items	56	$3.000	168.00	$3.500	196.00	$5.000	168.00
Daily balance reporting	1		100.00		75.00		125.00
Total charge for services			$446.85		$478.70		$516.80

Note: In this example, we use the Chapter 3 appendix data to construct realistic competitive bids for collection services from two banks (B and C) in addition to the existing pricing for the current provider, Bank A. A pricing spread of some $70 (or 15% on the lowest cost bank) for these services is not uncommon in a bidding situation.

Evaluating the RFPs

A comprehensive RFP can be as long as 20 pages. This much material can be daunting, but it's necessary in order to develop a level of comfort with the service provider. Can they in-

EXHIBIT 4-9 Lockbox Data Reported in Proposals				
Description	**Bidder A**	**Bidder B**	**Bidder C**	**Bidder D**
SERVICE CAPABILITY				
1 Lockbox implementation time	12 wks.	12 wks.	8–12 wks.	8 wks.
2 Disaster recovery	No third party back-up	On- & offsite back-up	Offsite service contract	On/ offsite back-up
3 Transmission security	No call-in	Log-on	None	Password; encryption
QUALITY				
4 Average tenure of processors	2 yrs.	3 yrs.	3.5 yrs.	2 yrs.
5 Dedicated service representatives	Retail pool	Retail pool	Assigned team	Assigned team
6 Error rate per 10,000 items	0.5	Did not know	0.87	1
PRICING				
7 Volume for price discount	At 50,000/ month	None	At 50,000/ month	At 25,000/ month
8 % ECR (bank)	3.0%	2.3%	3.1%	2.8%
9 Availability assignment	By item	Bank factor	Customer bank factor	By item

deed provide the service? Do they have a long-term commitment to the business? And finally, can the *musts* be met?

Musts will vary by organization and may include specific technological capabilities, years of experience, standards of customer service, and acceptable pricing. For example, in the light of the World Trade Center bombing and other incidents

EXHIBIT 4-10 Lockbox Selection Criteria/Measures of Performance			
Description	**2 Points**	**1 Point**	**0 Point**
SERVICE CAPABILITY			
1 Lockbox implementation time	<6 wks	6–12 wks	>12 wks
2 Disaster recovery	"Premium" service contract	Service contract/ own offsite	Own onsite or N/A
3 Transmission security	Callback/ encryption	Sign-on security	Passive/ none
QUALITY			
4 Average tenure of processors	>10 yrs.	5–10 yrs.	<5 yrs.
5 Dedicated service representatives	Individual assigned	Retail service pool	Retail/ wholesale pool
6 Error rate per 10,000 items	<1	1–2	>2
PRICING			
7 Volume for price discount	<25K	25–50K	>50K
8 % ECR (bank)	>3%	2-3%	<2%
9 Availability assignment	By item	Float factor by customer	Aggregated float factor

of international terrorism, some buyers may insist on specific disaster recovery plans such as off-site back-up procedures. Other buyers may demand dedicated service personnel and/or specific measures of bank or vendor performance. While some buyers continue to focus on price, it's clearly becoming only one of several critical concerns in the buying decision.

EXHIBIT 4-11 Lockbox Scoring Matrix					
Description	**Weight**	**Bank A**	**Bank B**	**Bank C**	**Bank D**
SERVICE CAPABILITY	30.0%				
1 Lockbox implementation time	150.0%	1	1	1	1
2 Disaster recovery	150.0%	0	0	1	1
3 Transmission security	100.0%	0	1	0	2
QUALITY	40.0%				
4 Average tenure of processors	100.0%	0	0	0	0
5 Dedicated service representatives	150.0%	1	1	2	2
6 Error rate per 10,000 items	200.0%	2	0	2	1
PRICING	40.0%				
7 Volume for price discount	90.0%	1	0	1	2
8 % ECR (bank)	20.0%	1	0	1	0
9 Availability assignment	50.0%	2	1	0	2
TOTAL WEIGHT ADJUSTED POINTS	100.0%	34.9	13.5	43.4	46.2

A first step in evaluating RFPs is to arrange a tabular listing by topic and response (see Exhibit 4-9 for selected responses to a lockbox RFP). To evaluate these data, each question should be ranked in importance (see Exhibit 4-10 for a hypothetical set of point values for selected responses). The resulting values are applied against weightings to develop a score for each bidder (Exhibit 4-11). Weights and point assignments can be adjusted once these preliminary scores have been calculated. (The weights and point assignments in our examples are entirely arbitrary and presented merely as an illustration). A full RFP may have 30 to 50 questions for each product bid, depending on the requirements of the various organizational functions (finance, systems, payables, and so on).

The RFI/RFP process is used by many organizations because it is an objective approach to the complex analysis of outsourcing alternatives. In addition to the obvious advantage of explicitly rating relevant variables, buyers can demonstrate the objectivity of their approach to their own management and to unsuccessful bidders. Developing selection criteria also assures that important decision factors won't be overlooked in the evaluation process.

·5·

Product Planning, Pricing, and Profitability Analysis

*Make no little **plans**; they have no magic to stir men's blood.*

—Daniel Hudson Burnham, Chicago architect
(1846–1912)

*I don't give a (expletive) what happens. I want you all to stonewall it, let them plead the Fifth Amendment, cover-up or anything else, if it'll save it, save the **plan**.*

—Richard M. Nixon (1913–1994)

This chapter will examine cashflow from the general view of both the balance sheet and the income statement. The chapters that follow will narrow this focus: Chapters 6 through 8 will review specific income statement elements and Chapter 9 will examine selected balance sheet components.

In accounting terms, cash is an asset, but in operating terms, cash directly affects and is changed by income statement components. We begin our financial statement discussion with a "macro" view of cash: the effect of *profitability analysis* on cash and the balance sheet.

■ TRADITIONAL PROFITABILITY ANALYSIS

Profitability analysis is an examination of price, volume, and the relevant cost structure for a product or service. Along with *product planning* and *pricing strategy*, profitability analysis is usually the responsibility of the manager of sales, marketing, or strategic planning. Despite the fact that profitability analysis requires financial expertise, this important function rarely involves the participation of any financial manager.

Profitability analysis nearly always exists in the corporate world as a historical reporting of completed events. Accountants and financial analysts review profits to report on completed fiscal periods or on specific projects. Financial analysts evaluate profits against equity (ROE), sales (return-on-sales), or assets (ROA), or against results from earlier periods. If profitability analysis is used at all in the planning stage, it's usually in strategic planning or marketing, areas geared toward investment rather than the careful consideration of costs, sales, and cashflow.

The IRR and the MCC

In corporate finance, cash inflows and outflows are often taken into consideration when analyzing the cost versus the return of a proposed investment. The cost is usually measured as *net present value* (NPV). "Present value" is the worth of a dollar today received or spent at a specific time in the future at an assumed interest rate. "Net present value" is the present value of the flows of cash netted to a single dollar amount, as valued at the company's cost of capital. A positive NPV is usually considered as sufficient to proceed with the proposed investment.

For convenience, many analysts use an alternative measure, the *internal rate of return* (IRR), that yields nearly the same result as the NPV. The IRR is that interest rate that makes the total of the present value of cash outflows and inflows equal. IRRs are convenient because they can be directly compared to the cost of funds: Both numbers are stated as percentage amounts. The cost of funds, or more correctly, the *cost of capital*, is the cost of using debt and equity capital to finance the activities of a business. It has two different uses, the marginal cost of capital (MCC) and the average cost of capital (ACC).

The *average cost of capital* is the current dividend, interest, and retained earnings cost of financing the business. The *marginal cost of capital* is the projected future cost of financing the business based on expected returns by the credit and equity markets. We will be using the MCC in the discussion in this chapter and the ACC in Chapter 9.

Despite the well established use of these methods in corporate finance, problems arise when they are applied to reengineering efforts:

- *Timing and causes of cashflows.* The IRR is typically calculated on the basis of annual flows rather than on a shorter period of time (daily, weekly, or monthly); the cash outflow or inflow is presumed to be spent or collected at the end of the year. The problem with this assumption is that cash is often spent early in period 1 and not received until late in that period or in subsequent periods. Such timing, as we will see in cases later in this chapter, can convert an acceptable target profit to a mediocre actual profit or loss.

    The IRR should be calculated on shorter than annual time periods in order to accurately reflect the actual inflows and outflows of cash. Yet even the fine tuning of IRRs does little to improve the quality of the data used. Who is to say that a cash inflow will really occur in year 2, or that it will be of a certain amount? Even daily intervals do not tell us much about potential problems or possible solutions. The cases presented in this chapter show that an inflow or outflow is caused by a multitude of factors.

- *Rate of return uncertainty.* The rate of return in financial markets is based on such varied economic factors as interest rates, the performance of the equity markets, industry and company profitability, and hundreds of other variables. An MCC assumption today has only limited relation to the MCC of tomorrow, despite the fact that many corporate decisions involve intermediate and long-term time horizons. Even if cash inflow and outflow projections are met as forecast, the IRR may be below the MCC by the time revenue begins.

- *Logic circularity.* IRRs calculate the return from a project based on assumptions about cashflows *prior* to proceeding with the investment decision. Similarly, MCCs assume that funds can be raised based on the profitability of the ongoing business, without taking into account the risk or uncertainty of the new project. The fact is that the profitability and cost experience of an existing portfolio have only a tangential relationship to new products, markets, and customers. The development of sales may take longer than was forecasted, and costs may turn out to be higher than were expected.

The real culprit is the timing of cash inflows and outflows as they relate to the cashflow timeline discussed in Chapter 2. To illustrate, Exhibit 5-1 shows a heavy equipment manufacturer with sales of $500 million per year and the following top portion of the income statement.

The result is a target gross margin of 10.5%, against which selling, general, and administrative expenses are charged. With invested capital of $250 million, the target return-on-equity capital (ROE) is 10% ($25 million net profit ÷ $250 million invested capital), a respectable return and well above the current 30-year U.S. Treasury Bond rate (about 6½%). Is it reasonable to assume that a new investment will generate equivalent profitability, cashflow, and ROE?

We'll see in the following pages how such assumptions can be incorrect.

EXHIBIT 5-1   Manufacturing Company Income Statement

			% of Sales
Sales		$500.0 million	100.0%
Less: Materials	$3XX million		
Labor	50 million		
Overhead	25 million		
Manufacturing costs		447.5 million	89.5%
Gross margin		$52.5 million	10.5%
Less: Sales and G&A expenses		27.5 million	5.5%
Net profit		$25.0 million	5.0%

■ CASHFLOW REENGINEERING PROFITABILITY ANALYSIS

Cashflow reengineering brings the skills of finance to the product planning and pricing process. We analyze the actual cash outflows supporting each sales activity to determine whether target returns can be achieved. The cases in this section are from a heavy equipment manufacturing company and two service businesses, a health insurance firm and a commercial finance company.

At the heart of profitability analysis is the concept of *opportunity cost*. Opportunity cost is the consideration of alternative uses for capital (or other scarce resources) currently invested in a production or service, with the normal alternative use frequently defined as the organization's cost of capital or cost of funds. Opportunity cost is analyzed by calculating the *realized gross margin*—the company's target gross margin minus timeline delays from extra work-days. (*Work days* is the count of days required to complete each timeline element.)

Put simply, the profitability of an activity should be measured against the cost of debt and equity investment necessary to fund the activity. Too often sales or product managers develop analyses without this perspective, and investments that appear moderately profitable in plans and budgets become significant losses in the real world of competition and cost overruns.

Profitability in a Manufacturing Company

Costs of manufacturing and invoicing do not include a calculation of the *time value of money*, that is, the "lost" income from company funds that are invested in materials, labor, and overhead during the manufacturing process. To analyze this critical but overlooked element, the various timeline activities of the heavy equipment manufacturer presented in Exhibit 5-1 are restated in Exhibit 5-2 as "work days" and "GM (gross margin) % impact."

These data indicate that while the target time to manufacture (including purchasing materials) is 165 days (or 5½ months), the actual time to manufacture and invoice is an astounding 270 days, or 9 months. These additional 105 days (3½ months) cause the gross margin percentage to decline from the target 10.5% to a realized 4.2%. After sales and general and administrative expenses, net profits become fairly slim (2.5% in this particular case), resulting in a return-on-capital of 5%. This is below the opportunity cost of either the 30-year Treasury Bond rate or perhaps 10+% using a realistic weighted marginal cost of capital.

In other words, any time the actual ROE falls below the relevant opportunity cost or cost of capital, the correct financial decision is to eliminate the product being manufactured and sold. The freed capital can then be invested in other projects (or in 30-year U.S. Treasury Bonds or to pay down borrowings). This is a basic tenet of managerial finance, that the return from a project (usually calculated as the internal rate of return or IRR) must exceed the cost of funds (the marginal cost of capital or MCC) for a project to be undertaken.

In presenting this analysis, the financial manager would emphasize the time value of money element of the working capital cycle. The opportunity cost of investing funds in manufacturing and invoicing a product has a significant impact on the target return (measured as the gross margin percentage)

EXHIBIT 5-2   Manufacturing Company Work Days and Gross Margin Impact (derived from Exhibit 5-1)

Detail of Income Statement	Work Days	GM%[*] Impact
Target gross margin	165.0	10.50
Less		
Materials (5–2a)	90.0	2.10
Work in process (5–2b)	74.0	1.75
Invoice preparation (5–2c)	60.0	1.40
Receipt of good funds (5–2d)	46.0	1.10
Total work days	270.0	
Equals		
Realized gross margin %		4.15

*GM% = gross margin percentage

from that product. Let's examine how this would occur at the micro level of a specific production process. All four Exhibit 5-2 timeline elements (listed as 5-2a through 5-2d) contribute to the length of the cycle.

Materials (5-2a) were purchased far in advance of production, due to pricing discounts from vendors and concern for access to dependable supply sources. Most of these purchases were speculative, however, based only partially on reasonable forecasts of customer needs.

The physical movement of materials through the work stations and the operations at each work station took longer than expected. These delays in manufacturing were reported on the income statement as work-in-process (5-2b). Investigation revealed that the shop layout was not sequential, causing inefficient movement between shop areas and buildings. Also, scheduling at each work station was overly complex, involving elaborate production activities and inspections.

Development of *just-in-time* (JIT) processes for materials and work-in-process improvement would help reduce these cycle times. JIT essentially means having the right materials, parts, and products in the right place at the right time, on the theory that excess inventory means waste and, as we have seen, cost. The basic tenets of JIT are few transactions, few "disturbances" (relying instead on periodic scheduling), the grouping of manufacturing cells (including equipment) to minimize travel distances, and a major emphasis on quality control (QC). QC is essential to avoid work stoppages and to minimize the need to hold buffer or safety inventory in case defective materials are found (see Chapter 7 of *Manufacturing Planning and Control Systems* by Thomas E. Vollmann, William Lee Berry, and D. Clay Whybark, 2nd ed., Homewood, IL: Dow Jones-Irwin, 1988).

Manufacturing data from various production work areas had to be collected and verified, and invoices had to be matched against contract requirements and limitations. These elaborate processes delayed invoice preparation (5-2c). A redesign of labor and materials management systems reduced data collection and review times and automated the invoice/contract matching process.

Receipt of good funds (5-2d) involves the entire cash collection cycle, from reviewing customer invoices and authorizing payments, to the banking of funds received. Treasury management improvements—such as lockboxing and electronic funds transfer—can shorten this processing time. As we noted in Chapter 3, the purpose of the lockbox is to hasten the processing of monies mailed to organizations. Banks intercept the mail at the post office and deposit checks received, reducing the mailing and clearing time ("availability") by one to two days. Converting from paper checks to electronic funds transfer also speeds the process.

> ⇥ **Electronic funds transfer** mechanisms include clearing payments on a same-day basis (Fedwire) and a next-day basis (ACH and EDI).
>
> The *Fedwire* system is operated by the Federal Reserve System, with payment sent by one bank and received by another on a same-day, final basis—that is, a payment sent cannot generally be recovered.
>
> With *ACH* (automated clearing house) transactions, an organization sends payment files to a bank that batches, stores, and then transmits the files electronically to receiving banks for credit to the vendors or

other payees the following day. Because the amount of data accompanying an ACH is limited, other larger data field formats, generically known as EDI, have become available.

EDI (electronic data interchange) is the exchange of computer-readable data between trading partners, including financial data for transferring funds. EDI transactions may include purchase orders and invoices as well as payments. EDI messages are transmitted through *value-added communications networks* (VANS), which act as electronic mailboxes to receive, store, and process messages. (EDI collection services are discussed in Chapter 6; EDI disbursement services are reviewed in Chapter 7).

It's clear that by redesigning the information systems involved in invoicing, using JIT, and changing various treasury management processes, total cycle time can be significantly reduced toward the target of 5½ months. Each of these opportunities must be investigated by the appropriate disciplines: The materials element needs input from purchasing managers; the work-in-process element should involve production managers; invoice preparation requires input from both production and invoicing managers; and receipt of good funds should be examined by receivables managers. All of this demands a degree of cooperation that's not customary in many traditional line-and-staff organizations. Lack of cooperation is often the cause of failure when target returns are not achieved.

Should these efforts prove unsuccessful and the actual gross margin percentage fall below the target, the only alternative may be to increase prices or abandon the product. Companies can use profitability analysis to plan the pricing and profitability of products and services or to determine the cause of failure to meet profitability targets. Obviously, it should be used more often in the planning stage. Companies need to determine realistic manufacturing and invoicing cycle times prior to the commitment of capital, and managers responsible for each element in the cycle should help make that determination.

Profitability in Service Organizations

Unlike manufacturing companies, service industries are quite dissimilar in their operations and their invoicing cycles. Each service industry has its own unique production processes, its own nomenclature, and often its own terms for settling transactions. The following examples illustrate proper analytical procedures.

In the insurance market, group health coverage is frequently provided as an administrative service (known as *ASO*, or sometimes *alternate funded business*) rather than as a traditional, fully insured product. The insurance company is engaged by the corporate client to provide coverage to its employees and to pay providers (hospitals, physicians) or employees as claims are settled. Any funds paid by the insurer are then reimbursed by the company, along with an additional fee for administering the claim service.

The insurance company in our example has a target of two days for average claim payments. These are held awaiting the replenishment of advances made on previously settled claims. This results in a target gross margin percentage of 0.65%, which, while appearing to be unrealistically low, is actually fairly significant compensation considering the limited role performed by the insurer—especially when applied against a $500 million annual cash flow. With invested capital of $30 million for that segment of the business, the resulting target return-on-equity is 10.8%. A financial analysis similar to Exhibit 5-2 is presented in Exhibit 5-3 and shows various problems.

The insurer made incorrect assumptions regarding its financial obligations and had an inadequate understanding of the necessary bank balances and fees required prior to reimbursement by corporate clients. Their target gross margin of 0.65% became an actual loss of 0.50%, even before sales and other general and administrative expenses were paid.

Timeline elements 5-3a through 5-3d each contribute to the length of the cycle—3.7 days versus the target of 2.0 days. Client funds advanced (5-3a) represents monies that have been advanced in expectation of claim payments to insureds or providers. Insurer bank fees paid (5-3b) represents the charges for maintaining bank accounts from which claims are

EXHIBIT 5-3   Services Organization Work Days and Gross Margin Impact (Insurance Company)

	Work Days	GM% Impact
Target gross margin	2.0	0.65
Less		
Client funds advanced (5-3a)	–0.7	–0.25
Insurer bank fees paid (5-3b)	0.9	0.30
Insurer bank balances advanced (5-3c)	2.4	0.80
Insurer ASO costs (5-3d)	1.1	0.30
Total work days	3.7	
Equals		
Realized gross margin		–0.5

paid. Bank charges are primarily for checks paid and wire transfers received (or other funding mechanisms).

Insurer bank balances advanced (5-3c) represents monies advanced by the insurer to cover claim checks issued. If these advances had not been made, insured and provider checks would not have been honored by the issuing bank. In all cases, the advance is repaid by the client company, but the insurer is out the funds for an average of 2.4 days. Insurer ASO costs (5-3d) are the various administrative costs of operating this business, including personnel, systems, and other expenses.

Potential areas of improvement include the following:

- Require corporations to provide reimbursement by Fedwire on the day that claims are paid, or require them to advance two to three days worth of funds prior to payment (based on data from the checks issued file)

- Pay claims off the company's bank account to eliminate the use of insurer funds

- Base reimbursements on issued (rather than paid) disbursements, which would allow 1+ days of additional funding to the insurer

Developing a profitable business requires a coordinated effort by marketing, systems, claims, and treasury managers to either reduce expenses or find additional revenues. If this does not happen, the result may be similar to that of our manufacturing company example: price increases or abandonment of the market. Many insurance companies writing health coverage have in fact stopped selling such insurance because of insufficient profitability.

Other Service Industry Analyses

Similar analyses can be used for other types of service organizations. In the commercial finance industry, for example, various types of loans are made to dealers selling vehicles and large equipment. The automobile industry refers to these arrangements as "floor planning." Because manufacturers expect payment on delivery to their dealers, the dealers finance the vehicles until they're sold.

Cost elements include the following:

- *Method of payment.* "Paid as sold" liquidates the loan as inventory is sold; "scheduled liquidation" repays loans based on specific calendar timing regardless of sales from inventory. Paid as sold is preferred by clients because repayments don't have to be made until inventory is liquidated (normally as retail sales). Scheduled liquidation is preferred by commercial finance companies because cashflows are "assured" on specific dates (assuming clients make the payments as contracted).

- *Interest charges.* Interest charges are set by formula, but may be negotiated with the client in order to win or retain business. These charges have a major impact on the realized gross margin percentage.

- *Late fees.* Late fees result from the failure to make timely scheduled liquidation payments based on contractual terms. Paid as sold payments are also subject to late fees if an audit reveals that inventory has been sold but timely payment has not been made.

- *Rebates of floor planning charges.* Manufacturer and distributors often rebate interest charges incurred by dealers to promote sales; these rebates are therefore shown as a negative calculation.

The profitability of specific deals, and of categories of deals by manufacturer, product, geographic region, and dealer will vary from the target gross margin, and will often lead to inadequate returns. In Exhibit 5-4 the target gross margin was 5%, but the actual gross margin was 2%, significantly below the business goal of the commercial finance company.

EXHIBIT 5-4 Services Organization Work Days and Gross Margin Impact (Commercial Finance Company)

Detail of Income Statement		Work Days	GM% Impact
Target gross margin		10.8	5.00
Less			
Method of payment	(5-4a)	4.5	0.75
Interest charges	(5-4b)	9.0	1.50
Late fees	(5-4c)	6.0	1.00
Rebates of floor planning charges	(5-4d)	−1.5	−0.25
Total work days		18.0	
Equals			
Realized gross margin			2.00

Timeline elements 5-4a through 5-4d contribute to the length of the cycle—18.0 days versus a target of 10.8 days. Areas of potential improvement include:

- More vigorous auditing of scheduled liquidation clients to ascertain that payments are made as inventory is liquidated (5-4a)

- Greater control in negotiating interest charges and other charges by sales (5-4b)

- Collection of appropriate late fees (5-4c)

Without these initiatives, the consequences may be similar to those of our previous examples: price increases or abandonment of the market. The lesson for commercial finance organizations is that every deal should have a required threshold of profitability to justify each financing agreement.

■ PLANNERS AND CASHFLOW REENGINEERS

Although product planning is one of the most important functions in any organization, it is often one of the most poorly managed. As we have seen in three situations taken from manufacturing, group health insurance, and automobile financing, plans are often based on unrealistic expectations for important cost elements. This is often due to the failure of marketing managers and planners to fully understand the cost dynamics managed by other functional areas.

Traditional capital budgeting procedures use data derived from existing financial statements, primarily profitability and the costs of capital, to project costs and returns for new investments. In contrast, cashflow reengineering analysis reexamines all pricing and cost assumptions within a business activity and encourages managers to make rational allocations of capital to deserving projects. Those projects are ones in which the actual return exceeds the opportunity cost. In this period of narrowing profit margins, it is essential to expand these techniques of cashflow reengineering in order to make better marketing and product planning decisions.

chapter

▪6▪

Collection Opportunities

*Put **money** in thy purse.*
—William Shakespeare (1564–1616)

***Check** enclosed.*
—Dorothy Parker (1893–1967), on her version of the two
most beautiful words in the English language

The collection segment of the cashflow timeline involves the receipt of cash from the sale of products or services. Unlike disbursements, which flow out through two primary channels (accounts payable and payroll), cash inflows can come from several sources, each requiring its own collection mechanisms and information systems. This chapter discusses a whole range of reengineering opportunities for collection flows, from the financing of sales to the banking of monies received at the completion of the collection timeline. Reengineering these activities reduces float and internal and bank/vendor costs, and generally makes the process more efficient.

➤➤ **Float** refers to any funds being moved into or out of a business. Collection float, discussed in this chapter, includes post office float, processing float, mail float, and availability float. Concentration float and disbursement float are examined in Chapters 7 and 8.

■ SALES FINANCING

Customers often need help in financing their purchases. In industries as varied as automobiles and office equipment, where customers are often unable to make large cash outlays for the purchase amount, sales financing programs—more than pricing or product features—often determine success or failure in making the sale. An illustration of a sales financing process was provided in Chapter 5, in the discussion of "floor planning" in the automobile industry.

Treasury managers involved in sales financing often develop pricing models based on timing of payment, anticipated fees (such as late payment fees), the cost of seller rebates, and the margin earned on finance charges over the cost of capital. In addition to the usual treasury and receivables capabilities, an in-house sales financing program needs the special skills of a credit group to analyze proposed transactions and of lawyers to prepare contracts and regulatory agency filings. Credit terms and interest charges must be determined (based on creditworthiness, asset life, and industry experience with credit) as well as specifications on how overdue payments will be dealt with.

An internal sales financing program can be a expensive to maintain, but it allows more direct control of response time and of the particulars of each "deal" being considered. Certain customers, given their business potential or cache, may deserve a coordinated sales financing effort, while others may be repeat business and require a less demanding effort.

The sales financing process can also be outsourced to a finance company or other lender. There are three possible formats:

1. *Full recourse* sales financing allows the lowest interest rates; the lender becomes the source of funds and offers advise on customer creditworthiness.

2. *Limited liability* or "ultimate-net-loss" limits the extent of the recourse, with the seller and lender each absorbing some credit risk.

3. With *no risk*, the lender independently determines the creditworthiness of the customer.

When lenders assume some or all of the risk, approvals can be delayed up to a few weeks, depending on the information provided by the customer and on his or her credit rating.

While an outsourcing program avoids certain credit group and legal overhead, it may adversely affect customer service. Certain lenders focus on transaction activity and may not understand the importance of service to the customers of the selling company. Problems might arise when questions are directed to the lender regarding such matters as the mechanics and crediting of payments.

■ INVOICE GENERATION

The process of generating invoices is often a shared responsibility of sales, receivables (credit), and systems, with critical decisions on the design and timing of the invoice cycle made at the convenience of systems managers. Frequently, invoice runs are inserted when time is available in the mainframe processing cycle, without regard to the optimal timing for printing and mailing. Some financial managers work with the various business units of their organizations to improve the invoicing process.

- *Improving invoice design.* Simplifying and streamlining the invoice eliminates superfluous information and multiple addresses. The invoice should be easy to read and to pay, with a clean look. A single return address forces the remitter to mail payments to the intended address rather than to an address that may delay processing. (One client had four addresses on each bill—the home office, the regional office, the office of the sales rep, and the lockbox address. Little wonder that many items were misdirected to the wrong location!)

  Invoice design may involve developing formats readable by automated equipment such as MICR and OCR.

  ⇥ **MICR** (magnetic ink character recognition) and **OCR** (optical character recognition) are fonts or print characters that have a distinctive design recognizable by reader-sorter equipment. MICR and OCR characters are printed in special ink at designated positions (usually at the bottom) on checks and remittance documents.

- *Improving the timing of the invoice.* We noted in Chapter 2 that substantial research has been conducted over the past decade examining alternative invoice mailing dates and the resulting payment "receive date" for both corporate and retail payments. For most industries, the best time for the customer to receive his or her monthly statement in order to make the payment by the due date is 25 days prior to the due date. Yet many companies are invoicing 10 to 15 days later than that, resulting in a DSO (days sales outstanding) that is longer than average for their industry. Similar results are found for industries billing on cycles other than monthly.

Invoicing Case: Steel Manufacturing Company

A steel manufacturing company billed $250 million per year by mailed invoices prepared through three information systems. Billing terms were "net 30," that is, payments were considered late if received more than 30 days after the invoice was received by the customer. Consistent with industry practice, no cash discounts were offered.

Weekly system runs printed invoices an average of 20 days after the sale date. The due date for payment was 30 days after the target date for the customer to receive the invoice. Given typical mail times in the geographic areas served by the company, customers received these invoices approximately 17 days prior to the due date. The following was a typical timeline sequence:

Sale of product:	February 1
Target issuance of invoice:	As soon as possible after February 1 (assume February 5)
Target customer receipt of invoice:	February 8
Actual issuance of invoice:	February 20
Actual customer receipt of invoice:	February 23
Target due date:	March 8
Actual due date:	March 23

The slippage or float lost between the target and actual due dates was 15 days. The value of these lost days, at an assumed 10% cost of capital, was calculated as $250 million ÷ 365 calendar days x 15 lost days x 10% cost of capital = $1.03 million. Our research determined that the delay in invoicing was caused primarily by scheduling issues within information systems: Invoicing cycles were run at certain weekly intervals at the convenience of the systems department.

Once senior management of the steel company became aware of the potential value of the lost float—in excess of $1 million a year—it was a relatively simple matter to convince the systems department to reschedule their processing runs. While some customers did notice the change in the timing of their monthly invoices and held checks until the usual release date, many paid once the bill was approved (see discussion, Chapter 8). The realized annual savings exceeded $500,000!

■ PRACTICES IN CASH COLLECTIONS

In the earliest form of collections processing, payments were directed to an organization's offices, where mail would be delivered mid-morning by the post office, opened, checks pulled and prepared for deposit, and a run to the bank made sometime in the middle of the day. Companies today often continue to process internally because of special handling requirements or very high volumes (usually in excess of 250,000 items per month).

There are numerous issues and problems to consider with this process.

- *Post office float.* Mail can sit in the main post office or in a branch for several hours, causing the delivery to be one or two days later than if the mail were picked up by the addressee. This occurs primarily in older, East Coast post offices, and in those situations were several sorts are necessary to assign mail to specific delivery routes. Such sorts may involve main city zip codes, street addresses, and post office boxes.

- *Collection float.* Collection float is comprised of *mail float* and *availability float.*

  ↠ **Mail float** is the time during which letters are in the mail delivery system. Mail float is reduced by having all mail directed to a lockbox in the main mail facility in each city and by arranging pick-ups as soon as the first sort is completed. This avoids secondary mail sorts and the delay of postal carrier delivery. Mail can be received by the lockbox as early as 5:00 to 6:00 A.M., with opening and processing shortly thereafter; this allows checks to be deposited long before the close of that day's ledger credit, discussed in Chapter 3.

➻ **Availability float** is the interval from the depositing of a check to the time the bank considers the funds cleared or "available." The banking system customarily assigns zero, one, or two day availability to all deposited checks that have been drawn on U.S. commercial banks. Checks drawn on savings banks, savings and loan associations, credit unions, and banks outside of the United States can take considerably longer to clear. Specific clearing times are determined by each bank; they usually reflect what the bank expects to receive in availability as it clears checks deposited.

The total of mail and availability days, or collection time, can be minimized by careful selection of the receiving destination. Certain cities have very fast collection times and are preferable to cities with longer times. Items processed internally by a company should be at the best sites for the management of float.

■ *Processing float.* Processing float refers to processing time within the company office.

➻ **Processing float** is the time interval from the receipt of mailed checks to the time of deposit. Bank lockboxes minimize such time by using dedicated processes to open envelopes, pull and copy checks, prepare deposit tickets, and enter the deposit into remittance processing.

Because mail may not be delivered until mid- to late morning, the deposit of checks received may not occur until after the close of ledger credit at the bank. This often occurs at branch banks, which must close early in order for the bank's courier to take checks to the main facility for processing. A branch may "close" at 2 P.M., while the main bank could be open until 6 P.M. or later. While convenient to the depositor, accounts at a bank branch may have a negative impact on processing float.

■ *Control issues.* Checks processed internally through the offices of a company may be stolen and cashed by employees. Customers will eventually complain about not receiving credit for payments, but months may pass while the thefts continue to occur. (See Chapter 10 for a more complete discussion of this issue.)

■ *Deposit bank issues.* Companies often choose their depository banks based on convenience or a credit relationship. The depository bank may be in the same area as the processing facility; it may offer mortgages at preferred rates to company officers; or it may put an ATM machine in the building and offer employees free checking. While all of these matters are important, the selection of a depository bank should be based on the fees charged and the availability granted.

Our consulting work has discovered situations where fees varied among candidate depository banks by as much as 5¢ per item, which is $5,000 per month if 100,000 items are being deposited. Variations in availability can be as much as one-fourth day. Time for ledger cut-off also varies considerably, depending on the location of the bank's processing center. If the bank's courier must transport deposited checks to a distant processing center, your deposit may have to be made as early as 2 P.M. for same-day credit.

■ COLLECTIONS REENGINEERING

Internal Improvements

There are a limited number of opportunities to improve internal collection practices. Unless the company processes in excess of 200,000 items per month, most authorities agree that outsourcing (lockboxing) is the best decision. The largest internal savings can be made by having a lockbox system handle office receipts and other such items. Also, alternative depository banks should be analyzed and redundant local depository accounts eliminated. Other internal improvement opportunities include reducing processing float, banking any monies received prior to the bank's close of business each day for deposit (ledger) credit, improving invoice design and timing, and converting from paper to electronic processing whenever possible.

Outsourcing

WHOLESALE LOCKBOX

The original form of cashflow reengineering through outsourcing was the lockbox, created shortly after the Second World War. The standard lockbox product was established to circumvent the delays inherent in office processing and to reduce opportunities for theft. In its simplest form—the wholesale lockbox—a company asks its customers to send their payments to a post office box. That box is monitored by the company's lockbox bank. The bank picks up the mail, brings it back to the processing center, and deposits the items into the company's account. The bank then notifies the company of the deposit totals and sends or transmits the payment detail information directly to the company.

Lockboxes improve availability by processing at night in order to make the critical deposit times for credit (usually the early morning hours), and by locating in cities with aggressive check clearing practices. For example, Chicago is generally considered an aggressive lockbox location; Wichita is not. A company would therefore be wise to direct payments to a bank lockbox in Chicago rather than in Wichita.

Beginning in the 1970s, banks and consultants began to develop analytical models to determine the optimum sites for the location of lockboxes. These models require data on standard mail times, bank availability, and the monthly pattern of checks sent to the company from various sending locations ("send points"). The data are analyzed to determine the optimal locations for lockboxes based on minimizing total collection time.

Current prohibitions against interstate banking were established in the McFadden Act of 1927. While various changes to branch banking limitations have been allowed, full interstate banking will occur in 1997. Wholesale lockbox networks overcome these current limitations by offering multiple collection sites through a single bank or vendor. With the network approach, collection sites in key cities receive and process mail and make deposits to local banks. The advantage is that a relationship with a single bank can give you multiple-site lockboxing; the disadvantage is slightly worse availability than would be achieved using different banks.

Wholesale Lockbox Case: Heavy Equipment Manufacturing Company A heavy equipment manufacturing company had been utilizing a wholesale lockbox system since the mid-1980s for accounts receivable payments. The system utilized three bank wholesale lockboxes, located in the Southeast, the Southwest, and the West Coast. In the early 1990s, competitive pressures and variations in product distribution patterns began to change its customer base, increasing business in the Southwest while reducing it on both coasts. A collection float study was undertaken to analyze the current wholesale lockbox system and evaluate alternative configurations for improved performance and/or reduced cost. The study was based on data from checks received at the company's current lockboxes during a 30-day period, analyzed by a lockbox model.

Exhibit 6-1 summarizes the sampled dollar volumes and item counts used in the analysis. All items under $5,000 were excluded as immaterial to the results, as were all items not meeting various edits within the model. These edits included missing data (such as zip codes), illogical data (such as checks mailed after the receive date), and checks too long in the mail (in excess of 45 days). With these exclusions, 74% of the dollars were left for analysis, representing 8% of the total items collected during the 30-day period.

The average collection time for the current system was found to be 3.44 calendar days. The disparity between this ob-

EXHIBIT 6-1   Current Lockbox System Volumes

Lockbox Site/Bank	$000	Items	Average $ per Item
Southwest bank	$34,260	5,476	$6,256
Southeast bank	$7,928	4,194	$1,890
West Coast bank	$3,518	1,986	$1,771
Sample Total	$45,707	11,656	$3,921
Studied Items Total	$33,766	884	$38,197

served time and the time of a redirected system was significant, about one-fifth of a day. The redirected system changed the wholesale lockbox addresses for customers to more appropriate locations assigned by the model and aggressively followed up on items misdirected by customers to the wrong lockbox.

The study showed that more than $25,000 per year in float could be saved (calculated as $240,000 at a 10% cost of capital + approximately $2,000/year for those items excluded by the analysis). The company could aggressively reassign or redirect remittances to the most appropriate lockbox by notifying its customers of the correct address for receipts, reducing collection time to 3.24 days.

The company's geographic distribution of customers indicated that the largest concentration (based on dollars) was in the Southwest (including Southern California), and selected states in other areas. Exhibit 6-2 represents data by sending location.

This heavy concentration in a single, broad geographic region, along with the very large dollar amounts (the average check studied was over $38,000), made it clear that the two low volume lockboxes could be eliminated without signifi-

EXHIBIT 6-2 Geographic Distribution of Send Points to Lockboxes (for States Greater than 2% of Studied Remittance Dollars)

Send Point	% of $ Sent
Texas	37.2%
California	18.6%
Nevada	13.9%
Missouri	8.7%
Arizona	6.6%
Oklahoma	2.2%

cantly affecting collection time (estimated by the model at 3.30 days). This would reduce the expenses of the current three lockbox system, and leave only one lockbox relationship to manage.

RETAIL LOCKBOX

A retail lockbox operates similar to the wholesale lockbox, with the added feature of being able to process MICR or scan-line characters printed at the bottom of the remittance document (usually the invoice) and the check. This makes processing faster and cheaper and reduces data entry errors caused by keying mistakes. Insurance premiums, credit card remittances, and utility bills can use retail lockbox processing because the payment usually matches the billed amount. Because most retail lockboxes involve these types of small dollar payments, float is typically not an issue in the selection process.

As companies redesign billing systems and invoices to accommodate standard payment amounts, the demand for retail lockboxing remains relatively strong. MICR technology can now print several data fields, including alternative payment amounts (such as the minimum acceptable amount, the total due, and various other choices) and data references (such as the account number and invoice number). Businesses generally prefer retail processing to wholesale processing for three reasons:

1. Significantly lower cost (about one-fourth the cost on a per item basis)

2. Lower error rate

3. Ability of the bank or vendor to provide a daily transmission of the processed data file, including all MICR and check data

Despite the demand, banks and vendors have been exiting this cash management service, primarily because of its very low profit margins. While wholesale lockbox services are very widely offered, there are only about ten reliable retail lockbox services nationwide. Businesses with monthly retail volumes in excess of 200,000 items should consider purchasing or leasing equipment for internal processing. It is usually cost effective to outsource to a bank or vendor when volume is below that amount.

IMAGE CAPTURE LOCKBOX TECHNOLOGIES

The lockbox systems described so far provide traditional processing, with remittance data for the cash deposit either keyed (if wholesale) or scanned (if retail) into the accounts receivable file. Newer systems use *receivables matching* and *imaging* technologies to update accounts receivable files.

Receivables matching involves periodic (usually daily) transmission of the accounts receivable file to the lockbox in a standard format. As cash is received in payment of open invoices, receivables are matched against each payment based on unique identifiers, such as account, order, or transaction numbers. When an identifier is matched with an amount paid, the receivable is considered cleared. If a match does not occur, additional invoice data is keyed to attempt a match, and unmatched items are sent to the company for resolution.

Benefits of receivables matching include:

- Fewer errors due to keying mistakes

- Faster collections updating to expedite the credit and collection process

- Access to a totally automated accounts receivable environment within the bank or vendor

An inefficient internal accounts receivable process will *not* be improved by use of receivables matching, however. A thorough review of current procedures is necessary prior to implementation, including the design of documents, the structure of the receivables file, and the processing of "exceptions" (where no match occurs).

Imaging technology takes an electronic picture of the check received and the remittance document, which can then be archived, retrieved, and transmitted to the company. Using a template of every type of remittance document received, the technology recognizes characters and converts them to electronic data that automatically updates the accounts receivable file.

The technology can also be used to expedite exception processing. The exception is imaged and transmitted to the company, which researches the item and returns it for the completion of the receivables updating. In large companies that receive many items without remittance documents, exception imaging can save days in collection cycle time—a considerable amount of float.

Because of the substantial costs of the technologies, receivables matching and imaging have not been widely used. Yet even though imaging is considerably more costly than standard lockbox processing, the value in time saved and the elimination of internal processing costs may make these applications appealing to certain companies. Imaging permits paper invoicing and checks to continue to flow between organizations and their customers, with the conversion of that paper to an electronic image once it reaches the processor.

ELECTRONIC COLLECTION PRODUCTS

The two primary electronic collection products were introduced in Chapter 5: *ACH* preauthorized consumer debits, used for insurance premiums, mortgage payments, and other collection cycles involving fixed amounts; and *EDI*, used for corporate trade payments. Their primary advantage is that they eliminate paper and its associated costs and time delays. They also enhance relationships between trading partners (primarily with EDI) and guarantee certain dates of payment. There is, of course, a cost to set up the electronic transaction systems, and a potential loss of float due to next-day transfer of funds.

Despite several years of promotion by banks and vendors, the volume of ACH and EDI is relatively small and—given the current bias of customers to pay by check—not likely to grow substantially. There are various reasons for this situation, including the refusal of customers to yield control over access to their funds, and concern that a debit will be for a charge in dispute. Successful applications of ACH have come at some expense to either the buyer or the seller. For example, insurance premiums are often paid by ACH debit because insurance companies either refuse to collect monthly premiums by check, or charge a hefty surcharge for the privilege, often 1 to 2% above the annual premium amount. Mortgages are paid by ACH either because borrowers receive a lower interest rate, often ¼%, or because it is a condition of the loan.

Banks are offering EDI collection products that allow customers to receive a single electronic payment for all invoices paid, supported by remittance advices in standard EDI formats. EDI volumes have remained trivial for corporate collections, however, primarily because companies want to control the date of release of payments and want a paper audit trail should a dispute occur. ACH and EDI will be revisited in Chapter 8.

Other types of electronic collections include *POS* (point-of-sale) terminal data transfer for credit and debit card consumer purchases, *Fedwire* transfers for same-day final payments (customary in certain industries, such as securities and real estate), and *net settlement* systems. Net settlement is used in the airline industry and transfers only the net amount owed on purchases and sales.

■ COST ANALYSIS OF INTERNAL PROCESSING AND OUTSOURCING

Outsourcing through the use of traditional lockboxing generally costs about 15¢ per item for retail processing and about 60¢ per item for wholesale processing. This does not include the costs of account maintenance, data transmission, and exception processing. Reliable estimates of equivalent costs for internal processing vary, depending on the efficiency of the process and on the volumes handled. Experience is too limited to cite retail internal costs for volumes under 200,000/month—nearly all these companies use bank or vendor lockboxes.

Internal processing of wholesale items will often cost $1 to $2 and will always suffer from poorer mail and availability times than a bank lockbox. A company will miss the morning deposit cut-off times available in a bank, and many companies don't operate in cities providing the fastest collection times. Placing collections in a lockbox also avoids the possibility of the theft of incoming cash by an employee. For all of these reasons, some form of lockboxing is almost always a better choice for a company than internal processing.

Given the widespread acceptance and the maturity of traditional wholesale lockboxing (now five decades old), opportunities for cashflow reengineering of the system are fairly limited. Even so-called small and medium-size companies (under perhaps $100 million in annual sales) now have access to lockboxing through community and regional banks. The major reengineering opportunities remain in the design and timing of invoices, the conversion to retail lockbox processing, and the outsourcing of receivables processing.

chapter

·7·

Disbursement Opportunities

Oranges and lemons,
Say the bells of St. Clement's.
You owe me five farthings,
Say the bells of St. Martin's.
*When will you **pay** me?*
Say the bells of Old Bailey.
When I grow rich,
Say the bells of Shoreditch.

—Oranges and Lemons, Nursery Rhymes

*I will gladly **pay** you Tuesday for a hamburger today.*

—J. Wellington Wimpy, in the comic strip *Popeye*,
E.C. Segar (1894–1938)

The disbursement segment of the cashflow timeline involves all the payments made by a business or not-for-profit organization. While specialized payments—such as claims paid in the insurance industry—offer significant opportunities for reengineering, this chapter will focus on reengineering the most common disbursement functions: *accounts payable* and *payroll.*

■ PRACTICES IN ACCOUNTS PAYABLE

Accounts payable managers struggle through mountains of paper and procedures to review invoices and purchase orders, determine if items have been received in good order, and attempt to issue payments in a timely manner. When performing these tasks, many accounts payable managers are driven by two conflicting objectives:

1. *The "clean desk" rule.* Bills are paid as received so long as appropriate authorizations and accounting codes are provided and supporting documents are attached. "Getting the work done" takes priority over concerns for cashflow and the value of float. In fact, payments are often made prior to the due date (usually 30 days from the invoice issuance date, or "*net 30*") and even earlier than industry practice, which is 5 to 20 days after the due date.

2. *The "pay slowly" rule.* Senior executives pressure accounts payable managers to slow payments in order to gain float, provided that supplier goodwill is not strained. As a result, according to Dun & Bradstreet data, *days sales outstanding* (DSO), the number of days between invoicing and payment, has gradually increased over the past five years.

This pay quick/pay slow dichotomy has forced accounts payable managers to evolve from the relatively mechanical function of paying invoices as presented and reviewed to managing cashflow, vendor sensitivity, cash discounts, new technology, and concerns for float.

In many companies, the accounts payable manager doesn't have the authority to create or enforce rules regarding purchases or to reject payment requests, except for specific cause. The function is essentially clerical, involving the review of authorized approval signatures and budget codes. Managers have no say in scheduling payments (except for those over a large dollar amount, say $50,000) or in making payments by electronic funds transfer.

The typical payables cycle involves the following steps:

1. Invoices are delivered to the accounts payable office or to the business unit that purchased the product or service.

2. The business unit prepares a voucher, indicating approval by signature and by recording the appropriate accounting codes. For invoices routed to accounts payable, the invoice is matched to an approved purchase order (P.O.) and receiving report. If there is no purchase order, the business unit is contacted to determine if the items were indeed ordered and received and to obtain the necessary codes for accounting purposes. If there is no receiving report, the receiving area is contacted to determine that the item was in fact received.

3. Checks are ordered by accounts payable using a check request form or direct systems input, and data is entered to the disbursement system. The check cycle runs in the disbursement system overnight.

4. Check originals are received the following morning and are either manually or facsimile signed. They are matched to a register for special handling instructions, including "pulls" for cancellation or for checks requiring accompanying documents.

5. Checks are mailed first class or couriered to the vendor, accompanied either by a check stub with supporting detail or by other material.

Accounts Payable Case: Diversified Services Company

A sample of recent accounts payable activity at a large diversified services company covered some $10 million in payments over a two-month period. The average *early* payment (using a target of 30 days) was 8 days of float for general vendor payables, worth about $20,000/year (at a 10% cost of funds, calculated as $10 million ÷ 365 days x 8 days of early payment x 10%). Each additional day of delay would be worth an additional $2,700. Individual payments greater than $25,000 are listed in Exhibit 7-1.

EXHIBIT 7-1   Sample of Accounts Payable Experience (Individual Payments >$25,000; Repeated Payees Deleted)

Payee (Industry)	$ Amount (000)	Days Paid Early[1]	Purchase Order[2]
Fleet/vehicle lease	488	17	N
Public power utility	285	15	Y
Building services	155	15	Y
Insurance services	150	2	N
Office equipment servicing	131	20	Y
Audio-visual presentation support	45	27	N
Office supplies	34	2	Y
Total Payments >$25,000 Number = 20	3134	12⅔	Y = ½ N = ½
Total Payments Number = 750	4416	8	Y = ⅔ N = ⅓

[1]Days paid earlier than 30 days, the standard credit period for invoices (as in "net 30").
[2]Was a completed Purchase Order executed prior to the expenditure? Y = yes, N = no

From the data in Exhibit 7-1, we see that management of the payments in relation to the due date was actually worse for large payments than for smaller payments! In fact, not a single large payment (greater than $25,000) was paid on or after the normal due date (day 30).

An analysis of purchase orders for the sample data indicated that close to one-third of all transactions did not have the necessary documentation, despite clear policies requiring purchase orders for all but emergency and convenience purchases (such as gasoline for fleet vehicles). Purchases typically accompanied by purchase orders included paper and bulk stationery, equipment maintenance and repair, and new capital and office equipment. Purchases without purchase orders included restaurants and hotels used for meetings and conferences, couriers, film developing, hardware and paint for maintenance, display exhibitors, temporary services, moving and transfer, and books and magazines. A close examination of these purchases without purchase orders indicated multiple vendors in each category, with a lack of volume pricing and, in some instances, premium pricing. Several payments were to vendors that no one could identify!

Purchasing had become a decentralized function, carried out at times by individual departments ordering directly from vendors and at other times by the purchasing unit. No statistics were available to quantify the cost of these practices and records were dispersed throughout the company. The fact that multiple payments were being made to the same vendors without audit or review indicated that the following opportunities existed:

- Quantity discounts for large volume purchases from a single vendor

- Standardization of products purchased

- Matching of items invoiced against items received

- Improved forecasting of purchases

- Determination of economic quantities for orders, that is, the appropriate number of items in each purchase

We recommended that all purchasing functions be centralized, including the negotiation of vendor prices and the issuing of purchase orders. Exceptions would be made for computer equipment, construction activity, and other specialized purchasing that required technical expertise.

The annual benefit eventually developed for the disbursement segment of the cashflow timeline was $2.5 million. This benefit assumed a conservative 5% savings for company purchases (exclusive of computer equipment and construction costs) and was calculated as follows:

5% savings on annual purchases of $56 million		$2,820,000
Less: Cost to establish purchasing department (5 personnel @ $30,000 salaries and benefits)	$150,000	
Manager	40,000	
Purchasing system	100,000	
Overhead, Space	30,000	−320,000
Net Annual Benefit		$2,500,000

Several steps were taken to centralize purchasing:

1. A company-wide survey was undertaken to determine the impact of centralized purchasing, exclusive of computers, equipment, and construction activity. At the same time, current purchasing procedures were documented and a list was made of frequently used vendors. Survey results indicated that nearly every business unit queried believed it was in a "special circumstance" and used that excuse to circumvent purchasing requirements.

2. A purchasing system was selected that allowed standardization of products, polling of approved vendors for quotes, and review/audit of invoices. (There are several widely used systems in the business community; some support complementary Accounts Payable modules.)

3. Purchase requests from business units were directed to the central purchasing facility. Each business unit was notified of specific procedures and locations, and follow-up was made with those units that continued to purchase directly from vendors.

■ PRACTICES IN PAYROLL DISBURSEMENT

Direct Deposit

Most organizations have evolved from making payrolls by currency to making payrolls by payroll check. More recently, *direct deposit* through the ACH to the employee's bank account has become an attractive alternative. In a direct deposit program, the employee submits a voided copy of his or her bank account check to the employer, and various data from the check (such as the bank transit routing number and the account number) are used to credit the account on payday.

For the employer, the primary advantage of direct deposit is lower cost. An ACH transaction is 10¢ or less, while a payroll check is generally estimated to be in excess of $1. A secondary benefit is reduced employee absence during the workday, as there is no need to leave the premises to deposit or cash the payroll check. Direct deposit is also helpful in fraud control (see Chapter 10). The major disadvantage in the electronic transfer of funds is a loss of float: The employer is debited at the same time that the employee is credited. Various studies indicate that the funding of cleared payroll checks is highest on the third business day after checks are distributed. A company with a $6 million biweekly payroll and a 25% increase in direct deposit would experience a float loss of some $45,000, as calculated in Exhibit 7-2.

In this situation, the annual loss of $45,000 in float would be measured against the 90¢ savings per payroll check. Assuming 8,000 employees, conversion of 25% to direct deposit would reduce the number of checks issued by 2,000 every two weeks, or about 50,000 checks per year. The resulting savings of $45,000 (90¢ x 50,000) would about offset the float loss, which is typical in these types of programs.

Although many U.S. companies have succesfully promoted the use of direct deposit, for most companies it makes up less than one-half of all pays. Many employees want to hide pay from a spouse or friend; others have no bank account or simply misunderstand the mechanics of the program. Aggressive promotion, assisted by bank marketing materials, can significantly increase employee participation.

EXHIBIT 7-2   Value of Float Loss from Payroll Direct Deposit (Assumes $6 Million Paid Biweekly; 25% Increase in Direct Deposit; Value of Float at 10%)

Days Clearing after Payroll Date	% of Dollars Cleared Each Day	Dollar/Day Value	Value of Lost Float
0	8	$0	$ 0
1	10	$15,600	1,560
2	16	$31,200	4,992
3	35	$46,800	16,380
4	16	$62,400	9,984
5	8	$78,000	6,240
6	6	$93,600	5,616
7	1	$109,200	1,092
	100		$45,864

Petty Cash

Some businesses maintain petty cash to accommodate check cashing and travel reimbursement for employees. Petty cash balances are often tens of thousands of dollars, with additional costs for delivery of cash, the operation of the cages, and bank coin and currency charges. We believe petty cash services should be terminated for several reasons:

- To save the value of the float on the cash balances
- To eliminate banking, courier, and administrative costs for the cages
- To avoid the risk of burglary against company employees

Many companies have eliminated petty cash facilities by replacing them with corporate credit cards and/or automated teller machines (ATMs).

Outsourcing Payroll

Companies handling their own payrolls should consider outsourcing these responsibilities to a payroll service company. These vendors provide a relatively low cost alternative to the high fixed cost of payroll personnel, equipment, and systems. Although savings will vary significantly depending on the number of state filings and the size of the employee base, typical annual savings are in the range of $25,000.

Electronic Disbursement Products

The initial use of EDI (see Chapters 5 and 6) was for disbursements to vendors by large corporate purchasers such as General Motors. After calculating time lags and the cost of the old purchase order/invoice/check system, these companies determined that by using EDI they could typically save in excess of $100 per purchase. Errors due to repetitive keying—affecting an estimated 25 to 50% of all documents—would also be eliminated. With EDI, transaction standards developed through the American National Standards Institute (ANSI) are used in the transmission of data between the payer and its bank. This data indicates that the file was received in good order or that errors were detected. Once the bank has accurate payment instructions and the acknowledgement process is complete, data and funds are sent on to recipients.

■ OPPORTUNITIES IN DISBURSING: INTERNAL IMPROVEMENTS

Internal improvement of the accounts payable function can be made by carefully reviewing and analyzing the invoice approval and authorization process. Dollar limits by approver should be determined (much like check signing approval or the release of wire transfers), as well as the appropriateness of expenditures (for example, no tickets for "charity" events unless approved by the chairman), and the adequacy of purchase order and receiving report documentation.

Multiple Vendors

When multiple vendors are used for the same product or service, the opportunity for volume discounts is lost. Why then does this practice persist?

- Business unit managers favor certain vendors for reasons that have little to do with the corporate mission (the vendor is a long-time relationship, the vendor is convenient).

- "Emergency" purchases are made for unexpected or unplanned events.

As consultants, we've occasionally observed multiple payments to the same vendors and multiple payments to different vendors providing similar products or services. Typical purchases made from multiple vendors include office supplies, catered events at restaurants and hotels, and display and graphic design. Consolidating these purchases usually results in volume discounts and improved customer service.

Phony Vendors

Organizations should secure vendor files by limiting file access to senior managers only. All too often fraudulent payments are made to phony vendors who have entered the vendor file surreptitiously through purchasing or accounts payable. When small repetitive payments of, say, $500 to XYZ Company occur, the fraud can go undetected for years. In fact, most frauds are repetitive diversions of relatively small amounts, rather than single large embezzlements.

Vendor names and addresses may not match file data precisely, and payables clerks will often change addresses in the vendor file to conform to the invoice. A purchaser in a business unit who may want to include an explanatory letter or a registration form with a payment check may request that the check be sent to him for delivery to the vendor. If he's dishonest, he could divert the vendor payment to a false address.

Because banks usually don't verify any of the data on the face of a check and use only scanline MICR information to clear them, safeguards against payables check fraud can be seriously compromised. Access to approved vendor files should be limited, and all vendors should be screened for legitimacy (with tax ID numbers, proof of a valid business activity, or other sorts of identification).

Payables Practice: Pay Date versus Due Date

A significant reengineering opportunity exists in scheduling the release of accounts payable disbursements. Payables managers should compare actual payables dates to due dates and develop a diary system to hold payments to the time most appropriate for release. The sensitivity of individual vendors to delayed payments should be taken into account, particularly when they're the sole source of critical materials and supplies (what economists call a *monopsony*) or where there are only a few sources (an *oligopsony*). The effect of later payment release on float should be evaluated, and there should be negotiation with vendors for payment through EDI or the ACH.

Published statistics indicate that days sales outstanding (DSO) in the United States varies from about 30 to about 60 days, depending on specific industry practice, with average DSO at about 45 days. Clearly, there is room for delay given current practice, but these are vendor relations and ethics issues that go beyond our discussion here.

Review of Invoices

All too often invoices are not properly reviewed. Authorized signatures and accounting codes may go unverified, and documentation may fail to support the payment request. If the accounts payable staff does not have easy access to an approved signature list, check requests may be accepted or rejected solely on the basis of adequate accounting code data. Although many companies have authorized signature lists, few purge them regularly, leaving obsolete approval signatures from long-departed signers. In general practice, an up-to-date, approved signature list should be readily available to the accounts payable staff. This would allow them to ascertain that signatures match and prevent fraudulent actions by those requesting payment.

Organizations also often fail to provide dollar or purpose constraints to check requests. The following language from a company's policies and procedures manual is not uncommon: ". . . any company officer [or any officer with the title of Assistant Vice President and above] may approve a check request in any amount." An interesting example we noted at one company was a request processed for $750 for a golf and dinner outing. The accounts payable unit had no authority to deny this request and was required to complete processing as long as the appropriate codes were entered on the form. Good practice is to limit spending authority both by amount and purpose, based on the title and function of the corporate officer.

■ OPPORTUNITIES IN DISBURSING: BANK AND VENDOR PRODUCTS

Various bank and vendor products, including *controlled disbursement* and *account reconciliation*, can assist the financial manager in administering the purchasing and payables functions.

Purchasing/Payables Systems

Cashflow reengineering of purchasing and payables is often hindered by the limitations of older mainframe systems. For example, many systems cannot diary payables for release on a specified date ("35 days after receipt of invoice"), or organize vendors by purchasing frequency and price per item, or feed into systems for electronic data interchange (EDI). These are often batch systems, driven by tape and written in computer languages no longer fully supported, such as COBOL and FORTRAN. These systems often contain hundreds of "fixes," many essentially "hard-wired;" any further adjustments may require examination of thousands of lines of programming code—*if* qualified programmers can be found!

A further concern is the "century-dating" problem. These older systems will be unable to accommodate the date change beginning with the year 2000. Programs are currently being developed to adapt twentieth century dates to the twenty-first century. Century-dating will directly impact any routine that compares two dates to begin a work task ("SHIPPING DATE = 05/07/96; INVOICE DATE = SHIPPING DATE + 10 DAYS"). Estimates for replacing these systems vary widely depending on the information requirements of the organization. One of our consulting clients determined that the cost of modifications to its existing mainframe was approximately $7 million, and that a fully tailored replacement system probably exceeded $10 million!

"Off-the-shelf" purchasing and payables packages appear to be the most viable solution. A variety of these are available (from vendors such as Oracle Systems, Computer Associates, and ASI) at far lower cost than writing a new, customized system. These packages offer a number of useful features:

- Scheduling of all accounts payable to the appropriate check release dates

- Automatic crediting of cash discounts for early payment

- Easier management of multiple vendors for similar products

- Fewer purchases made without requisite purchase orders or other authorization

- Disbursement of payables through ACH, EDI, or other electronic payment programs

- Elimination of any duplicate payments sent to vendors in error (which can occur whenever invoice copies rather than originals are used to document payment)

- On-line inquiry capability, reducing the need for manual file searches (for compliance with tax filings and tax audit requests, for example)

- Possible interface with telephone system to automate payment inquiries

- Accurate and timely information to control payments and manage cashflows

- Payment of travel and entertainment reimbursements by ACH credit directly to employees' bank accounts, eliminating the need to issue individual disbursements.

Controlled Disbursement

The typical corporate disbursement account, similar to your personal checking account, requires sufficient balances to cover clearing checks. Because it is something of a guess as to precisely when checks will clear, balances are left on deposits that are "idle." Personal accounts earn a nominal interest rate (about 2% in 1996), while corporate checking accounts receive an ECR (earnings credit rate). The ECR can be applied to the purchase of bank services, but is typically worth much less than alternative opportunities for earnings.

The Federal Reserve Board, responsible for much of the check clearing activity in the United States, aggressively manages *clearing float* (the time required for checks to clear once deposited). Checks are cleared when they're delivered in what is called a "cash letter presentment" to banks. The Fed uses multiple daily cash letter presentments and improved transportation routings to minimize the clearing time.

A *controlled disbursement account* allows you to take advantage of the Fed system's efficiency by offering morning notification of the total amount of check clearings for that day against the corporate account. Controlled disbursing eliminates idle balances in the bank and lets the financial manager know the day's funding requirement by mid-morning.

Full Account Reconciliation

A supplement to controlled disbursement is full account reconciliation ("recon"), which automatically matches issued and cleared (paid) items monthly. Reports are sent to financial managers regarding exception items, which include the following:

- *Issued not paid.* Checks that have been written but haven't cleared. Many issuers research these checks after three months have passed, and corporations acting as fiduciaries (trustees of the funds of others) must remit such monies to the appropriate state agency after a specified period of time has elapsed (usually six years). This process is called "escheatment".

- *Paid not issued.* A check presented to the bank for payment but never entered on the corporate issued file. The omission may have been inadvertent, as can occur when a check issued in a branch office is not recorded in the main disbursement system.

- *Stop payments placed and removed.* A "stop" is made when it's determined that an error has occured in issuing a check, or when a check is lost or never received by the payee. The bank constructs a stop file to monitor clearing items, stops items matching the file description, and returns them to the depositor through the check clearing system. Any stop removal requires a company action, and is monitored to prevent legitimate stops from being terminated.

- *Force posted items.* Identical check sequence numbers. This shouldn't occur if checkstock is preprinted by a check printing company. Duplicate check sequence numbers may indicate questionable activity, such as attempted check fraud with counterfeit checkstock.

Regardless of the size of your organization, full reconciliation is worth the cost, usually a few cents per item. It avoids delays in performing reconciliation, removes the possibility of collusion between personnel issuing checks and those reconciling the checks, and eliminates the cost of the staff required to perform the reconciliation.

Procurement Cards

The procurement card is a special form of a credit card, issued through a bank or vendor to designated managers who occasionally need to make local purchases. The card eliminates the paperwork inherent in purchasing and payables systems, provides daily electronic information on transaction activity, and controls use through various codes embedded in the card technology. These codes impose limits on the amount per transaction, the number of transactions per card, and the types of purchases permitted. Any unapproved purchase will be rejected when the card is presented to a merchant for payment. The organization receives consolidated purchasing statements, in electronic or paper format, which summarize all transaction activity.

The major advantages of a procurement card program include the following:

- *Savings.* Users of procurement cards report that costs are significantly lower (perhaps one-half or more) than the formal purchase order/approval process managed by a purchasing department. The primary savings come from reduced paperwork, labor, and postage. If used with a large number of purchasers and vendors, however, the opportunity for volume discounts and supervision over vendor quality and service is considerably diminished.

- *Employee empowerment.* When given the power to make small purchasing decisions in their jobs, employees report a significant psychological benefit.

Disadvantages of the program must also be considered:

- *Entrenched opposition.* Purchasing department managers inevitably oppose procurement card programs because they see them as a threat to their roles and positions in the organization. This problem has no simple solution other than to solicit support from internal audit, the business units using the program, accounts payable, and, if possible, from senior management.

- *Tax reporting.* Procurement card reports do not provide adequate tax information for each purchase, such as whether taxes were paid and the amount of those taxes. While enhanced point-of-sale software will eventually remedy this problem, currently only a small percentage of credit card terminals have such capability. Most companies manage this problem by having taxes charged on all purchases and reporting this approach to the taxing authorities. Local governments' position on tax payment practices for procurement cards is unclear at this time (see "Purchasing Cards Trip Over Tax Reporting" by Michael T. Smith, Beverly Porter, & Jack Cantrell, *Corporate Cashflow*, Sept. 1995, pp. 21–22).

■ OPPORTUNITIES IN DISBURSING: OUTSOURCING

The complete outsourcing of disbursement processing has become increasingly popular in recent years. Payment is initiated by the transmission of a file to the selected bank through a VAN (an electronic value-added communications network— see Chapter 5). File formats include standards such as ANSI 820 (an EDI protocol) and custom formats directly from the company's payables system. Banks can issue payments the day following receipt of the file, but usually the payments are held until the appropriate release dates. When the disbursements are presented for payment, the company is notified so the daily clearing amount can be funded. All cleared items are reconciled, and appropriate summary and detail information is provided.

In other words, the entire process of managing disbursements is handled by the bank, with the corporate customer simply advising on exceptions once the payment file is prepared. Payments may be made in any form acceptable or desired by the recipient, including checks and electronic transactions in ACH, EDI, or Fedwire formats, and in several of the major currencies. Check payments are laser printed on blank safety-paper stock, eliminating the need to order and warehouse preprinted checkstock. Remittance advices are transmitted to the bank in an agreed-upon format, printed by the bank, and attached to the check. Current technology permits logos, signatures, and other nonstandard data to be printed on the check and remittance advice.

Advantages of disbursement outsourcing include the following:

- *Postage.* The bank can take the maximum postage discount allowed by the U.S. Postal Service. In 1996 that's as much as 4½¢ less than regular first-class postage. To qualify for this discount the Postal Service requires a high volume of mail to each receiving zipcode. An organization sending 2,500 disbursements per month, consisting of perhaps 1,000 accounts payable checks and 1,500 payroll checks, would save more than $1,000 in annual postage costs.

- *Check signing.* With current technology, authorized signatures can be digitized into the computer system of the bank. This eliminates the need to physically sign checks or to safeguard signature plates used on check signing machines.

- *Special messages.* Messages can be inserted on the check and/or on the remittance advice, such as "duplicate check" or, for payroll checks, "Ask about payroll direct deposit." Promotions and information can be changed each time checks are issued.

- *Local check printing.* Checks often need to be issued locally, such as in a branch office, or on an emergency basis after the file has been transmitted to the bank for processing. Current desktop technology allows users to issue such "emergency" checks and to transmit an issued file to the bank to be included with disbursements processed in the normal manner.

- *Access to electronic disbursing.* Many organizations are intimidated by the technology of electronic disbursement (ACH and EDI transactions involve protocols, value-added networks, encryption, and other data transmission requirements). Banks offering disbursement outsourcing can provide complete access on a "turn-key" basis to these electronic payment mechanisms; the only requirement for the corporate payor is to indicate the desired payment method in a specified field in the file.

- *Changes in bank accounts.* Corporate customers may want to add or delete disbursement banks due to changes in business, conflicts with current banks, changes in bank management due to merger or acquisition, or other factors. If checks are internally prepared, some preprinted checkstock will inevitably remain when these changes are made; also, lingering uncleared checks may force the account to be held open for lengthy periods.

  A more complex problem is the transfer of electronic transaction system feeds from the current bank to the new institution. Banks providing disbursement outsourcing allow checks to be issued on any bank and can accommodate such changes quickly and painlessly.

- *Security issues.* The bank accepts full responsibility for the security of the disbursement so long as their controls and file transmission protocols are observed. The corporate customer need not concern itself with stolen checkstock, altered checks presented for payment, or other possible breaches of security. This topic is covered more extensively in Chapter 10.

■ COST ANALYSIS OF INTERNAL PROCESSING AND OUTSOURCING

The cost of managing an internal disbursement operation depends on the extent of internal automation, the volume of disbursements, and the number of disbursing locations. Costs can vary substantially. Credible analyses we've reviewed show internal costs ranging from $1.50 to $8.00 per check, including all internal, banking, and mailing costs. Banks offer disbursement outsourcing for about 60¢ per check, and significantly less for ACH and EDI transactions (usually 10¢ to 30¢). The appendix to this chapter provides a template for developing an estimate of internal costs.

Outsourcing is most attractive with volumes in excess of 1,000 disbursements per month because it requires a fairly extensive implementation process; existing procedures must be converted to file formats that can be transmitted to the bank on a daily basis. Despite the size of this task, the potential for significant benefits is clear. A savings of $5.00 per disbursement on a volume of 25,000 transactions equals $125,000 saved annually. Savings will also be made by eliminating certain fixed costs, such as check printing and the check signing machines. Large organizations issuing in excess of 10,000 items per month are likely to save less per transaction due to efficiencies in their current internal process, but still the total annual benefit of outsourcing may be well into six figures.

■ ■ ■

CHAPTER 7 APPENDIX

INTERNAL COSTS TEMPLATE
FOR DISBURSEMENTS

The elements in an internal cash handling process include computer time and other equipment, including service contracts; labor; materials; warehousing; and overhead. In addition, essential costs paid to banks or vendors must be considered, including postage and banking costs. The template on the next page is a guide to selected costs that should be considered in developing a comprehensive check disbursement cost.

Type	Description	$/Unit	Unit	Volume	Vol Unit	$/Yr	$/Unit
Computer	Computer processing	2	/Job	500	Jobs/Yr	1000	0.02
Equipment	Burst/signing	50	/Mo	12	Yr	600	0.01
Labor	Acct reconcilement	16	/Hr	1.125	Hr/d	4500	0.08
Labor	Review and sort	16	/Hr	0.5	Hr/d	2000	0.03
Labor	Agency back office	10	/Hr	0.6	Hr/d	1500	0.03
Labor	Check research	13	/Lookup	525	Lookup/Yr	6825	0.11
Labor	Sign and bursting	16	/Hr	0.5	Hr/d	2000	0.03
Labor	Sort and distribute	16	/Hr	0.375	Hr/d	1500	0.03
Labor	Check control process	16	/Hr	16.5	Hr/d	66000	1.10
Labor	Check preparation	10	/Check	916	Chks/Yr	9160	0.15
Labor	Treasury analyst	17.5	/Hr	0.3	Hr/d	1312	0.02
Maintenance	Service contract	218	/Mo	12	Yr	2616	0.04
Material	Checkstock	40	/K cks	145	K Cks/Yr	5800	0.10
Material	Envelopes (correspondence)	50	/K env	20	K Env/Yr	1000	0.02
Material	Envelopes (window)	50	/K env	100	K Env/Yr	5000	0.08
Material	Remittance documents	5	/K sheets	125	K Sh/Yr	625	0.01
Overhead	General overhead	750	/Mo	12	Mo/Yr	9000	0.15

Type	Description	$/Unit	Unit	Volume	Vol Unit	$/Yr	$/Unit
Printer	Laser printing	0.02	/Page	60000	Pages/Yr	1200	0.02
Warehouse	Storage - forms type	200	/Form/Yr	0	Forms	0	0.01
Warehouse	Withdrawal	5.15	/Request	0	Req/Yr	0	0.01
	Subtotal (In-House)			60000		203363	2.05
Bank	Service fees (fixed)	150	/Mo	12	Mo/Yr	1800	0.03
Bank	Service fees (variable)	0.36	/Chk	60000	Cks/Yr	21480	0.36
Postage	Postage (regular 1st class)	0.34	/Env	40000	Env/Yr	40000	0.34
Postage	Postage (overweight)	0.55	/Env	20000	Env/Yr	20000	0.55
	Subtotal (Bank/Mail)			60000		83280	1.28
	Total			60000		286643	3.33

chapter

▪8▪

Cash Concentration and Banking Opportunities

Up and down the City Road,
In and out the Eagle,
That's the way the **money** *goes _*
Pop goes the weasel!
—Attributed to W. R. Mandale (about 1853)

Take the **money** *and run.*
—Woody Allen (1935 –)

The banking and investment of collected monies prior to disbursing them for expenses (such as payables and payroll) is called *cash concentration.* This chapter will discuss several concentration activities, including administering bank compensation, managing bank relations, forecasting cash, and using outsourcing services such as sweep accounts and investment management.

■ MANAGING CONCENTRATION AND BANK BALANCES

Most large organizations that collect and bank receipts through the procedures discussed in Chapter 6 do not have a lot of readily accessible cash on hand. Most likely, it is in a number of scattered bank accounts and remains there unless it is concentrated to a few large operating accounts. As we discussed in Chapter 5, the most common methods for concentration are wire transfers and ACHs.

Wire transfers move funds from collection accounts to concentration accounts on a same-day basis. ACHs are used to move funds on a next-day basis (monies moved one day are usable the next business day). Although wire transfers are about 100 times the cost of ACH transfers, they should be considered when collection banks receive more than $20,000 each day. These banks should be given standing instructions to wire any funds collected each day in excess of a predetermined amount. With collection banks that receive less than $20,000 each day, the concentration bank should prepare ACHs for each collection bank, send them through the ACH system, and receive the collected funds the next day.

Once cash is in a concentration account, the financial manager must decide whether to leave the balances for liquidity and safety, invest, or pay down outstanding debt. Obviously, the balances should not be used if the amounts are relatively small, if they are needed to pay the bank for its services, or if there are large outstanding disbursements to be honored (see Chapter 7). Balances may also be needed to compensate a credit relationship or to pay for cash management services through the ECR (see Chapter 3 Appendix).

Bank balance credits through the ECR have long been accepted as an important method of bank compensation for several reasons:

- Corporate DDA (demand deposit account) balances are liquid and immediately accessible for business needs.

- Balances are "soft" dollars, not budgeted or closely reviewed by senior management.

- Late cash in the corporate account, such as from wire activity, may earn more from an ECR credit than from a late-day overnight investment.

- The bank may require balances to support a credit line or a cash management service.

- When services are paid by fee, some banks bill a surcharge (though this is becoming increasingly rare due to competitive pressures).

When interest rates rose in the late 1970s, the value of balances left at banks began to exceed the ECR received. Financial managers started paying for services in fees and managing down balances to minimal amounts. Yet even today our reviews of thousands of bank statements and account analyses indicate that many idle or unused balances still remain. If these are no longer being used as a source of business funding, their value at the long-term cost of capital (probably more than 10%) could be substantial.

The financial manager may be able to find out the company's balance position through a recorded announcement over the telephone, but the limited detail of these recordings has encouraged many larger businesses to receive data through the modem of a personal computer. The typical PC report, called the *balance reporter*, includes the following information:

XYZ Corporation
Balance Reporter for Bank A
As of 15 NOV 9X
Currency USD (Dollars)
Account No. 34567

Ledger Balance	$250,000
Collected Balance	225,000
1 Day Float	25,000
2 or More Day Float	0
Total Debits	26,000
Total Credits	119,000

The *account analysis*, described in Chapter 3, is the monthly invoice that a bank presents to its corporate customers (see Chapter 3 Appendix for a definition of terms and an illustration). In a single statement, it summarizes the daily balance positions for the previous period, showing ledger and collected balances and other detail. All of the various charges incurred during the period are included; the example in Chapter 3 Appendix shows charges for account maintenance, deposited items, returned items (those not honored by the drawee bank, probably due to insufficient funds), checks paid (disbursements), and ACH paid items.

The financial manager should regularly compare these charges against those of competing banks; if they're high, the manager should negotiate for lower prices or choose another bank. While most of the charges presented in the Chapter 3 illustration are relatively competitive, certain charges, such as 13½¢ for ACH items, are well above the market price. The best way to determine competitive pricing is to visit with your bankers to comparison shop.

The Banker Visit, *or* Guess Who's Taking You to Lunch?

A consulting relationship with your banker can be extremely helpful to your reengineering effort. Bankers are an excellent source of information on cash and credit issues; they can recommend products to improve internal cashflow and explain how outsourcing services may be of help. A good banker will ask probing questions in order to fully understand your organization's products, services, markets, competition, regulatory constraints, and staffing issues. Only with time and effort can any outsider understand the problems of your business and suggest ideas to help run it more effectively.

Unfortunately, this kind of in-depth consulting relationship between corporations and banks is rare. The typical banker visit is more of a sales call, with him or her asking what's new at the company, followed by a pitch for the latest product or service being marketed by the bank. In order to make it attractive for you to take the necessary time, these visits often occur over lunch or in some other entertainment venue. This is a costly way to do business; company information can be better gained from databases and publications, and bank product information can be distributed at exhibitor booths and through advertising.

Bankers are under tremendous pressure to visit and to sell, and given current expense control programs, these visits must be as effective as possible. The banker's compensation is often based on the sale of product, either directly through commissions, or indirectly, through salary increases measured by performance (sales and/or the number of calls). Because the banker is rarely trained or motivated to probe for problems and opportunities, very little real consultation takes place.

In the past, financial managers had time to meet with bankers to describe current problems and developments within their organizations. With current downsizing programs, however, financial managers are often performing the jobs of two or even three people, and simply don't have the time to spend on unproductive banker visits. The result is that fewer banker appointments are accepted by companies, and there's less tolerance for wasting time. Both parties urgently want the process to be more efficient.

One way to help make it more efficient is to have a list of questions for your meeting with the banker. Typical questions you may want to ask include the following:

- *Pricing changes.* Will cash management prices be changing during the coming period? Banks often "forget" to announce price changes, hiding them in the monthly account analysis. This is an excellent opportunity to develop competitive pricing data on the services you use.

- *Organizational or strategic changes.* Is the bank planning to abandon certain businesses or types of clients (those outside its target market as defined by size, geography or type of industry)? Also, is the bank "in play" as an acquisition candidate? Your banker probably won't know, and neither will your stockbroker. Do your own homework, research per share market price versus *book value* (assets less liabilities, or net worth), published in the daily newspaper, *American Banker.* You should be concerned if your bank's market-to-book ratio is well below the average for its peer group of banks.

- *New product developments.* Has the bank developed an innovative approach to a difficult treasury problem of yours? An example would be a service that allows you to outsource receivables and payables to the bank once you establish transaction files (as discussed in Chapters 6 and 7).

- *Industry and competitor developments.* Are any of your competitors clients or prospective clients of the bank? If so, the banker may be a useful source of non-confidential market intelligence, or of information on industry groups and conferences.

Bank Fees and Balances Case: Hospital/HMO

A hospital and health maintenance organization (HMO) kept an average of about $500,000 in its two banks because it failed to understand the value of those balances. A 3% ECR credit on the balances helped compensate the banks for services, but if they had paid for those services in fees and invested the collected balances overnight (at an assumed rate of 8%), the company would have realized an annual benefit of $25,000 ($500,000 x [8%–3%]). (The 8% rate is based on the organization's expected average cost of capital; see Chapter 9).

We analyzed five bank services used by the hospital/HMO: retail and wholesale lockbox, check disbursements, wire transfers, and ACH debits and credits. Charges and item counts were aggregated to establish the cost of each service by bank. These costs could then be compared to industry averages to reveal potential savings, as shown in Exhibit 8-1.

The retail and wholesale per item lockbox charges at Bank A were 20¢ and 60¢, respectively. Industry data showed that the average per item charge for retail lockbox services with roughly the same volume level was 10¢, and that the average per item charge for wholesale lockbox services was 50¢. Comparing these costs to the charges for collection services at other banks in the company's location made it clear that the hospital/HMO could negotiate more favorable pricing for several bank services.

The per-check disbursement costs were 25¢ at Bank A and 35¢ at the hospital/HMO's other bank, Bank B. In the market at large, disbursement pricing averaged approximately 15¢ per item. Similarly, wire transfer and ACH costs at the two banks were above typical market charges. Negotiating these costs down to those of competitive banks saved the hospital/HMO $675/month, or over $8,000/year. The total an-

EXHIBIT 8-1	Analysis of Hospital/HMO Banking Costs				
Bank Service	Volume	Bank A	Bank B	Competitive Bank Pricing	Potential Savings
Retail lockbox	1,500	20¢	NU	10¢	150.00
Wholesale lockbox	1,000	60¢	NU	50¢	100.00
Check disbursements	750	25¢	35¢	15¢	112.50
Wire transfers	100	$10	$7.50	$6.00	275.00
ACH debits/ credits	500	20¢	15¢	10¢	37.50
Potential Monthly Savings					$675.00

NU = Not Used

nual savings from more aggressive bank balance and fee management approached $35,000.

■ CASH FORECASTING

The Daily Cash Position

The daily cash position can usually be determined at the start of the business day, when the bank sends balance report data to the organization. The report tells the financial manager what the company's bank balances were at yesterday's close of business. The financial manager should compile these balance totals into a spreadsheet of current cash activity, showing the day's beginning cash, expected collections of cash, and expected disbursements of cash. Cash collections and disbursements may occur regularly (daily lockbox receipts for products sold, payroll) or irregularly (a tax payment or the purchase of a major asset).

Once these various data are assembled and a projected closing position for the day is calculated, the financial manager can decide whether to invest excess funds, pay down outstanding debt, or do nothing (and allow any cash balance to pay for bank services through the ECR credit). The majority of businesses, including many manufacturing firms, are "cash poor"—for much of the year they are borrowing to finance inventory and other expenses in anticipation of future sales. Because the cost of their borrowing will exceed any possible investment return by three or four percentage points, these organizations normally pay down debt as cash becomes available.

Insurance companies, utilities, governments, and any companies with a dominant market position are generally "cash rich." These organizations should forecast cash requirements over the next one to two months to determine the appropriate maturity of any investment made with excess cash. For example, if it's determined that enough cash will be received to fund foreseeable disbursements over the next month, any cash surplus can be invested for that month, earning a higher yield than would repeated overnight investments.

A *yield curve* displays the different interest rates for investments of different maturities. The normal shape of this curve is upward because investors, anticipating future inflation, demand a greater return as maturities lengthen. In periods of normal (upward-sloping) yield curves, the difference between an overnight and a one-month investment on U.S. government equivalent debt will be somewhere between one-fifth of a percentage point (20 basis points) to one-fourth of a percentage point (25 basis points). (A *basis point*, or *bp*, is 1/100 of a percentage point). Longer investment maturity also avoids the repeated transaction costs of overnight investing—as much as $10 or more for each buy or sell trade. Total annual savings through accurate forecasting on a $1 million portfolio would be more than $30,000:

$1 million x 20–25 bp =	$2,000–$2,500
22 business days x $10 for each buy transaction =	$220
22 business days x $10 for each sell transaction =	$220
	$2,500–$3,000
x 12 months =	$30,000–$36,000

Of course, this strategy always contains a certain amount of risk. The organization may unexpectedly need cash, forcing a potentially embarrassing liquidation of the one month investment. If interest rates have risen, the security may also have lost value. The risk of significant loss is small, however, particularly if the investment is of high quality and traded during a period with a relatively stable yield curve.

The Cash Forecasting Process

Many cash forecasters accept information provided by sales, purchasing, or other functions without sufficient concern for the quality of that data. Even worse, many organizations simply pull down the day's bank balances, determine cash disbursements from check clearing data and expected wire transfers, and invest the balance overnight.

The sad truth is that the financial staff usually communicate only with their banks and with each other, so that the data on each day's activities has no meaning beyond the debits and credits on paper. If sales receipts decline or payables exceed expectations, the financial staff won't be alarmed—why should they be? If cash deficits continue and eventually fall below the expectations of senior management, someone will eventually take notice.

This actually happened to a client of ours. One division in this decentralized company decided that a vendor's price discounts were too attractive to pass up. The only "catch" was that huge purchases were needed to obtain the discounts. The division authorized the purchases despite the uncertainty of future sales and the need for new capital. The company didn't discover the situation until accounts payable notified finance of impending wire transfers to the vendor!

Few organizations use the resources and input of other departments to develop quality cash forecasting data. The typical financial manager knows little about the sales process, about who the important customers are and what they're buying, or about how the purchasing/payables cycle really works. They do know that receipts are collected and disbursements made, because these appear in the organization's bank accounts. What they don't know is what's behind these processes—what drives or causes these events.

A variety of statistical techniques are available to help forecast cash. The choice of a specific procedure is based on the timeframes under review:

- *Cyclical forecasts.* Forecasts exceeding one year are used to develop financial strategies for issuing debt and equity, and for rationing capital among alternative projects. The *percentage-of-sales method* makes predictions based on anticipated levels of sales, while *regression analysis* develops strategy based on a number of independent variables.

- *Seasonal forecasts.* Forecasts of one month to one year are used to determine how cash may be affected by seasonal influences or the monthly cycle of a business. It can also be used to determine the effect of adjustments in the collection or disbursement process—for example, the effect of delaying certain transactions by a number of days due to an impending cash shortfall. A valuable technique for seasonal forecasting is the *cash budget*, which can be used to determine the monthly status of cash, to arrange for cash sources, or to postpone expenditures.

- *Daily forecasts.* Forecasts of less than one month are used to calculate the immediate (overnight) cash position and to help determine the organization's response. There are two basic procedures for such forecasts: *cash scheduling* and the *distribution method.*

Detailed explanations of cyclical and seasonal techniques can be found in any standard statistics or finance text. What follows is a basic explanation of cash budgeting, cash scheduling, and the distribution method.

CASH BUDGETING

The cash budget is a list of projected monthly cash activity, with the timing of receipts and disbursements based on historical patterns. To illustrate, let's look at a company with net sales of $20,000 in June, $30,000 in July, and $25,000 in August. Its cash collections are 25% the month of the sale, 65% in the month after the sale, and 10% in the second month after the sale. Purchases are limited to 75% of that month's sales, and payroll is fixed at $2,000 each month. The cash position at the beginning of June is $6,000, and the desired level of cash is $5,000. This simplified scenario produces the cash budget shown in Exhibit 8-2.

This cash budget analysis suggests that there is ample cash available during the company's June to August period, and that there may be an opportunity in August to invest nearly $10,000 in surplus cash. The only problem with these conclusions is that they don't take into account intra-month variations, which can be fairly significant (see the Distribution Method example). The financial manager who relies solely on a monthly cash budget may find him- or herself overdrawn at the bank on particular days during the month.

CASH SCHEDULING

Cash scheduling uses a fairly simple methodology to establish a schedule of expected cash collections and disbursements. Each receipt or payment is individually estimated based on data collected from the business unit with responsibility for

EXHIBIT 8-2 Illustrative Cash Budget			
Cash Budget Activities	**June**	**July**	**August**
Net sales	$20,000	$30,000	$25,000
Cash collections	20,000	24,000	27,750
First month	5,000	7,500	6,250
Second month	*12,000	13,000	19,500
Third month	*3,000	*2,500	2,000
Cash disbursements	17,000	24,500	20,750
Purchases	15,000	22,500	18,750
Payroll	2,000	2,000	2,000
Cash gain (loss) during month	3,000	(1,500)	7,000
Beginning cash balance	6,000	9,000	7,500
Total cash balance	9,000	7,500	14,500
Desired cash level	5,000	5,000	5,000
Surplus (deficit) cash	4,000	2,500	9,500

*Data developed from sales in previous months

that particular receipt or payment. For example, the sales department may supply data on expected collections by date, while accounts payable may specify expected payments to vendors.

THE DISTRIBUTION METHOD

The distribution method is a more formal approach to the daily cash forecast; it assumes that there are repetitive patterns of cash receipt by day of the week and day of the month. To discern the patterns, actual receipts are compiled for two or three months. These receipts are then analyzed as a percentage of total monthly receipts by business day of the week and by business date of the month.

The analysis may reveal that the organization experiences its highest level of mailed receipts on Mondays (typical for much of American business) and a fairly even distribution the rest of the week. The analysis may also show a high collection day on the first and fifteenth business dates of the month, with no particular pattern during the remainder of that period. The specific factors are provided in Exhibit 8-3.

Assume that, based on the percentage-of-sales or regression methods, revenues for April, 199X are forecast at $3½ million. The fifth of April, a Wednesday, would be business day 3 of the month. The factors for that date would be 15% (day of the week) and .05 (day of the month). The day of the week is divided by the "par" (the amount if daily flows occurred evenly throughout the week). Using the business day concept, par is 20%. This quotient is then multiplied by the day of the month factor. The result of this is then multiplied by the expected revenues for the month, or, as a surrogate, the revenue experience of the preceding month (as long as no corrective factors are needed for delayed receivables or other changes). For the organization in our example, the forecast cash inflow for April fifth would be $131,250, calculated as (15% ÷ 20%) x .05 x $3½ million.

EXHIBIT 8-3 Day-of-the-Week and Day-of-the-Month Factors

Day-of-the-Week Factor		Day-of-the-Month Factor*	
Monday	30%	1st, 15th	15%
Tuesday	20%	2nd, 16th, 22nd	6%
Wednesday	15%	3rd, 14th, 17th	5%
Thursday	20%	4th, 18th	4%
Friday	15%	5th, 6th, 9th, 13th, 21st	3%
Weekends	0%	All other days	2%

*Business (not calender) day

Once regular collection inflows are forecast, the financial manager adds anticipated non-regular inflows (such as proceeds from new financings or from the sale of equipment) and subtracts outflow projections. These are usually based on daily forecasts of check clearings, or on the controlled disbursement presentment, along with any nonregular payments such as payroll, taxes, or debt repayment.

Cashflow Forecasting Case: Hotel and Resort Company

A hotel and resort company had sales of $600 million and total assets of $200 million. Five percent ($10 million) of the assets were made up of cash and U.S. government-equivalent investment securities of less than one year's maturity. They also had a credit line at a major regional bank to cover emergency and seasonal cash needs. The short-term holdings were managed by a Finance Committee, comprised of the CFO, the Treasurer, and the Comptroller, with advice by the company's banker. Short-term holdings included:

Cash in banks	$1,000,000
Overnight investments	2,000,000
Investments of 1 month maturity	1,000,000
Investments of 1 month to 6 months maturity	3,000,000
Investments of 6 months to 1 year maturity	3,000,000

Although the resort industry experiences seasonal fluctuations in business activity, this company enjoyed steady revenues because its properties were diversified throughout many locations. Using the distribution method, the average $50 million in monthly revenues were plotted against past day-of-the-month and day-of-the-week records. The day-of-the-week and day-of-the-month factors used in the example in Exhibit 8-2 were assumed for this example, reported in Exhibit 8-3. The results for the month of September 199X showed that the net position fell below $1 million only three times all month: a negative $539,100 on the 10th, a negative $2,918,246 on the 19th, and $593,602 on the 30th.

Because the balances on all but these three days were adequate for the company's liquidity needs, it was clear that significant savings could be gained by moving excess cash from short-term investments to longer-term holdings. Overnight investments could be eliminated, and $2 million could be held in cash. The other $1 million held overnight and the $1 million held in one-month maturities could be invested longer, perhaps for six months, with a resulting 50 bp and 30 bp gain, respectively. A 50 bp gain on $1 million is worth $5,000 annually (assuming these patterns continue throughout the year). Six-month investments could be sold prior to the expected negative balances in order to fund these amounts. Furthermore, cash now in six-month investments could more confidently be held in one-year securities, worth another 30 bp in additional yield.

By moving its short-term portfolio into longer-term investments, the hotel and resort operator was able to save $25,000 annually through higher interest returns and lower transaction costs. In addition, better forecasting convinced its bankers to lower the costs of the credit lines it provided the company.

■ OPPORTUNITIES IN CONCENTRATION: OUTSOURCING

There are two primary methods of outsoucing the concentration function: *sweep accounts* and *investment management/ advisory services*. Both products have become particularly important due to the downsizing of financial staff, which has reduced the amount of time and personnel available to pursue overnight and longer-term investment alternatives. In addition, given recent pressures to reduce costs, corporate support has declined for financial market information services (Reuters, Telerate) and similar expenditures.

Sweep Accounts

Offered by banks and securities firms, a *sweep* is an investment mechanism that automatically, at the close of business, moves balances from corporate accounts, invests the funds overnight, and returns the investment to the accounts the following morning. Interest is calculated and paid daily on the invested balances. Sweeps currently involve some $30 billion in daily activity. Their popularity is due to several converging pressures:

- *Cost of daily transactions.* Companies are recognizing that every daily investment decision—for wires or internal transfers, for the purchase or sale of a security—involves a transaction cost. They also realize that the Fed's 10% required reserve on balances earns no ECR credit (see the discussion in the Chapter 3 Appendix).

- *Financial institution promotion.* Banks and securities firms are now actively marketing families of inexpensive sweep products, despite their negative impact on bank deposit balances. Bank balances earn an ECR that is well below a bank's cost of funds, and so is an inexpensive source of capital for the bank. Banks today can manage their balance sheets and derive income from sweep products (now estimated at $300 million per year), with typical fees of about 50 bp on swept funds. The various sweep alternatives, often managed as money market funds, include U.S. government instruments, repurchase agreements (repos), and commercial paper. Offshore sweeps (for example, Eurodollar deposits in non–U.S. financial institutions) offer attractive interest yields unaffected by Federal Reserve requirements.

- *Sweep innovation.* The ongoing development of sweep products offers attractive new alternatives to traditional investments:
  - *Intra-day sweeps* optimize interest yields in the prime late morning time period.
  - *Tiered sweeps* send predetermined amounts to overnight funds and the balance to a long-term U.S. government fund with higher yields.
  - *"Real time" sweeps* use available funds for intermittent funds investment.

- *Lower short-term interest rates.* Short-term money rates have declined in recent years, with federal funds (money lent at standard rates between commercial banks overnight) falling to between 5¼% and 6% over the past 12 months. To invest at optimal rates, decisions have to be made by late morning—even though funds may be credited to a DDA any time during the day. Most financial managers have decided that with such low interest rates, the marginal gain from direct investments isn't worth the effort.

When considering sweep products, consider these issues:

- What is the collateral supporting the sweep? Remember that sweeps are not Federal Deposit Insurance Corporation (FDIC) insured. Are you comfortable with the quality of the investment?

- What are the mechanics of the sweep and when does it take place? Most accounts are swept after the close of business (often as late as midnight), but the sweep can also take place during the business day. Is a minimum sweep amount required? Are there other sweep restrictions?

- What is the bank's charge for the sweep? Charges can be on a fee basis, on a per transaction basis, or deducted from the interest rate credited. Typical fees are $125 to $250 a month. A $2,000 per year charge for a sweep is not unreasonable, considering the cost of idle bank balances, transaction charges per investment, management time, and systems costs.

Investment Management/Advisory Services

Investment management and advisory services have been available for many years to manage investment portfolios for corporate clients. Unlike long-term investors, such as institutions and individuals, businesses with excess cash tend to invest short term, up to six to twelve months. The primary reason for a short time horizon is the avoidance of interest rate risk, the potential for fluctuation in the portfolio value due to changes in long-term interest rates.

Recent studies indicate that, despite low price inflation, recent volatility in the long-term Treasury bond was 3½ times that of bond price volatility in the 1960s (see "Stock and Bond Risk: Forget What You Know," *Business Week*, July 8, 1996, pp. 108–109). This development has caused long-term investors to seek the relative stability of the stock market, with bond funds receiving about $10 billion in funds in 1996 versus $140 billion for stock funds! The current instability in fixed income investments has been attributed to the deregulation of banking, more active management of bonds through the use of derivatives, and the failure of the Federal Reserve to adjust short-term rates to the economic forces of the financial markets. In this environment, corporate investors are deciding to stay relatively short term in their placement of excess cash.

The majority of corporate investors use mutual (money) funds to outsource investment management, which involves the purchase of shares in a diversified, professionally managed portfolio of securities. Very large corporate investors often prefer to hire investment advisory services to manage their funds, permitting greater control over strategy and portfolio maturity, and the opportunity to negotiate fees.

The primary reasons for outsourcing this function are as follows:

- *Individual investor syndrome.* Unless the corporation manages a portfolio in excess of $10 million, it will often receive worse data and higher commission rates than professional money managers. In essence, it will treated as if it were a small investor. This is also seen in typical fee differentials for professional advice can be substantial, with $10 million portfolios paying 100 bp or more for management advice and $1 billion portfolios only 5 to 10 bp. Finally, small corporate investors may be excluded from attractive investment opportunities, such as IPOs (Initial Public Offerings) and Private Placements, investments sold to a limited number of investors and not SEC registered.

- *Competition in portfolio performance.* Outsourcing permits the investor to place funds with several managers, to develop a performance competition, and to calculate results based on the risk characteristics of the portfolio.

- *Cost.* The cost of external investment management is typically substantially less than maintaining adequate internal resources. A $25 million portfolio may cost 20 bp or about $50,000 to manage, costs that may be exceeded by those of even a minimal internal financial staff, investment data services and overhead. A mutual fund invested in short-term government instruments will cost from about 50 to about 75 bp in management fees, and those with longer-term debt holdings will typically have a somewhat higher fee structure.

- *Simplicity.* Mutual funds are available to businesses that meet the most basic investment requirements. A business must provide such data as form of ownership; place of organization; method of investment, such as initial and/or periodic deposit or exchange from another fund; and certification by an officer of the company that a board of directors resolution approved the investment. As of year end 1994, businesses held about $85 billion in money market funds, with fiduciary investors (e.g., trusts, estates) at about $350 billion and retirement plans at about $250 billion of all institutional investors (*Mutual Fund 1995 Fact Book*, Investment Company Institute).

  Investment management and advisory services are somewhat more complicated, in that a formal agreement is required requiring legal review, along with decisions on acceptable investment instruments and maturity. Banks have established investment pools through their trust departments for the management of short-term funds, using short-term investment funds (STIFS) and similar products.

The complexity of short-term investment options demands professional advice if yields are to be maximized on investable funds. In addition to obligations of the U.S. government (Treasury Bills, Notes, and Certificates) and the highest creditworthy corporations (commercial paper), acceptable investments for many portfolios include those listed in Exhibit 8-4. Should an investment manager or advisor be engaged, it is essential to establish appropriate investment guidelines to minimize inappropriate management actions. Exhibit 8-5 lists several critical areas for such guidelines (In addition, see the discussion on risk in Chapter 10.).

EXHIBIT 8-4 Securities for Short-Term Investment Portfolios	
Type of Security	**Description**
U.S. Government Agency Securities (but not backed by the full faith and credit of the U.S. Government)	Securities issued by such agencies as the Farm Credit System, the Federal Home Loan Banks, the Federal National Mortgage Association, and the Government National Mortgage Association.
Certficates of Deposit	A certificate representing a time deposit, an interest-bearing deposit at a banking institution with a specified maturity.
Eurodollar Certficates of Deposit	A certificate of deposit issued (usually in London) by a banking institution located outside of the United States
Bankers' Acceptances	A draft or bill of exchange used in international commercial transactions accepted by a financial institution, providing a guarantee of payment.
Yankee Certificates of Deposit ("Yankee CDs")	A certificate of deposit issued in the U.S. market by the branch of a foreign bank, payable in dollars.
Short-Term Credit Facilities	A participation by the investor in a short-term borrowing arrangement with corporate borrowers.
Repurchase Agreements ("Repos")	An arrangement where financial institutions sell securities to the investor and agree at the time of sale to repurchase them at a specific time and price, frequently the next business day.

EXHIBIT 8-5   Categories of Investment Guidelines

Category	Examples
Credit quality as measured by standard rating service evaluations	Triple A to B for long-term instruments; A1P1 to A2P2 for commercial paper
Average portfolio maturity to assure liquidity	6 or 12 months
Expected returns given the established benchmark rate	Fed funds + 25 bp (for a 6-month money market portfolio)
Investment instruments permitted	Government instruments; commercial paper; stocks of designated qualities
Approved investment managers	Specific firms
Authorizations for company investment actions	Trade orders; accounting; compliance

■ ANALYZING THE COSTS OF INTERNAL PROCESSING AND OUTSOURCING

Sweep accounts and investment management services offer economic alternatives to managing investments internally. Sweeps allow companies to obtain attractive overnight money market rates on bank balances without having to spend time determining the daily cash position and arranging for the placement of excess funds. Because checks that are being cleared in the account are being invested during the banking day, sweeps can also replace controlled disbursement. Sweeps reduce staff time to manage the account, lower balance reporting charges (sweeps are automatic), and avoid overdraft charges (which occur whenever you're in a negative position with your bank).

The primary *internal* improvement opportunities are in bank fee and bank balance management, and—for organizations with very large cashflows—in forecasting. We've developed significant benefits for companies by reducing bank fees, eliminating excess balances, and replacing expensive banking services with lower cost alternatives (such as ACHs for wires). Typical annual savings can be tens of thousands of dollars.

chapter

·**9**·

Balance Sheet Issues

*So far as my coin would stretch; and where it
would not, I have used my **credit.***

—William Shakespeare (1564–1616)

*Too caustic? To hell with **cost**—we'll make the
picture anyway.*

—Samuel Goldwyn (1882–1974)

The balance sheet is the "structure" in which the assets, liabilities, and capital of an organization reside. Any reengineering effort must assure that this structure is properly organized to maximize cashflow efficiency and minimize underproductive assets. We'll first take a look at the structure of the balance sheet and then review the management of working capital.

■ THE FINANCIAL STRUCTURE

In Chapter 5 we discussed cost of capital issues, focusing on the use of the MCC (marginal cost of capital) in investment decisions, sometimes called "capital budgeting." A related concept is the *ACC*, the *average cost of capital*, which is a basic tool for managing the balance sheet structure. The ACC is the cost of financing the business, weighted by the amount of debt (borrowings) and equity (stock) on the balance sheet.

To illustrate how the ACC is calculated and used, let's look at a company with $50 million of assets, funded half by debt and half by equity capital.

The average cost of the company's debt capital is taken directly from its interest payments for bank loans, bonds or other sources of long-term borrowings. We calculate the cost on an after-tax basis, using the maximum corporate tax rate of 34%. Assuming a debt cost of 7½%, the average cost of debt capital is about 5% ([1 – 34%] multiplied by 7½%).

Short-term borrowings (less than one year) should also be included in the calculation of the average cost of debt capital. Unlike the rate for long-term debt, however, the short-term rate is often variable. It's usually pegged to the Prime Rate, or "Prime" (the rate banks charge their preferred customers), which changes periodically, the LIBOR (the London Interbank Borrowing Rate), or Federal Funds rate (the borrowing/lending rate charged between commercial banks), which changes every day. To keep things simple, we'll ignore the cost of short-term debt in this discussion.

The average cost of equity capital is more difficult to determine. It's the sum of the cost of dividend payments and the cost of the expected growth of the business in retained earnings or in the value of the company's stock (normally measured over one year). If our company is on the New York Stock Exchange, it may pay a 4% dividend to shareholders, who also expect a 10% increase in the price of their stock. The average cost of equity capital is therefore 14% (4% for dividends + 10% for expected growth). No adjustment is made for taxes because dividends are not deductible business expenses.

With average debt capital at 5% and average equity capital at 14%, the ACC will be 9½%, calculated as follows:

	% of Total Capital		After-Tax Cost		Cost for Each Type of Capital
Debt	50%	X	.05	=	.025
Equity	50%	X	.14	=	.070
Total Cost					.095

We can now ask whether 50% debt/50% equity is the optimal balance sheet structure for the company.

A creditor's judgment of the mix of debt and equity of a business will depend on the industry, the maturity of company management, the competitive position of the company, and other factors. Often the most important element, however, is the amount of debt on the balance sheet. Because a business encumbered by interest and principal payments on borrowings is less likely to be able to repay new debt, creditors tend to favor companies relatively free of any existing fixed obligations. The cost of debt capital will be lower with a 0% debt/100% equity mix, and considerably higher as the amount of debt increases.

Based on this understanding, we can estimate the cost of capital at 25% increments of debt, as displayed in Exhibit 9-1.

The 50% debt/50% equity ratio does yield the lowest ACC for this company, even though the 0% debt/100% equity scenario, with the lowest individual cost of capital components, may have appeared, before the analysis, to be the least expensive choice. Continuing with this procedure, the financial manager can attempt to calibrate the exact debt/equity ratio preferred by the marketplace, perhaps 40% debt/60% equity, or 45% debt/55% equity, or even 55% debt/45% equity, depending on the cost of adding another "chunk" of debt or equity financing. Although 0% debt/100% equity reduces explicit debt and equity costs and gives the business a very high credit rating, the goal in structuring the balance sheet should be to optimize the debt/equity mix. This is reflected in current

**EXHIBIT 9-1   Average Costs of Capital
at Varying Percentages of Debt**

Before-Tax Cost		% of Capital		After-Tax Cost*		Cost for Each Mix of Capital
6%	Debt	0%	times	.000	=	.125
12½%	Equity	100%		+ .125		
6¾%	Debt	25%	times	.016	=	.117
13½%	Equity	75%		+ .101		
7½%	Debt	50%	times	.025	=	.095
14%	Equity	50%		+ .070		
9½%	Debt	75%	times	.071	=	.121
20%	Equity	25%		+ .050		

*The average cost of debt capital is based on the marginal corporate tax rate (1 – 34%) times the debt cost. The after-tax cost is calculated as the before-tax cost times the percentage of capital for each balance sheet component.

corporate balance sheets: Standard & Poor's reports that only 1% of all companies rated in 1995 received a Triple A rating, the highest available, down from 2% in 1994. Only 22% of all companies rated received an A or higher in 1995.

Financial Leverage

During the 1980s, financial "players" often did damage to the balance sheet structure and to shareholder value when they aggressively used the borrowing power of assets to buy and sell companies, whole or in pieces. This technique, known as *financial leverage*, uses debt to finance business deals on the expectation that resulting profits will exceed the cost of the debt. Companies could afford to overpay because interest rates were falling; they knew the cost of money would be less at the time of the transaction than when the deals were planned. They also knew equity values were rising, so selling pieces of a company separately would fetch more than selling the company whole. This financial game largely ended by 1990. Today, stable cashflow is a critical element in the financial structure of a business.

Forbes Magazine defines financial leverage as long-term debt (including leases) divided by total capitalization (long-term debt, common and preferred equity, deferred taxes, investment tax credits, and minority interests in consolidated subsidiaries). Exhibit 9-2 shows median financial leverage (debt-to-capital) ratios compiled by the magazine (January 1, 1996, pp. 234, 237) for twenty industry aggregates. The all-industry median is 33.1%, which means that on the typical balance sheet (at least among larger companies), debt represents one-third and equity (including retained earnings) represents two-thirds of all financing. Capital-intensive industries such as aerospace, transport, financial services, and energy are the heavy users of debt; the lighter users are either regulated to a higher level (insurance) or are highly profitable and not in need of frequent borrowing (computers and communication).

Our 50% debt/50% equity company does exist, in financial services such as brokerage and commodity firms, leasing and finance, and in such other sectors as airlines, supermarkets (due to land, building, and equipment costs), and textiles. In large companies, concerned with rating agency opinion for the issuance of debt or equity, financial managers try to find that mix where the ACC is minimized and access to "investment grade" investors—those willing to accept A or Triple B ratings—is assured. The market for "junk grade" debt, below Triple B, is much smaller and more expensive and should be avoided.

Managing the balance sheet to minimize financing costs can have a significant impact on cashflow. If the mix of our $50 million company were 25% debt/75% equity instead of 50% debt/50% equity, each percentage point of additional cost would equal an annual expense of $500,000, or over $1 million a year. If the company becomes over-leveraged during a business downturn, the debt won't be serviced and the company might not survive. If the company is under-leveraged and operates at less than maximum financial efficiency, it may run into serious problems with shareholders.

EXHIBIT 9-2 Financial Leverage Ratios by Industry	
Industry (and number of companies)	**Debt/Capital**
Food distributors (53)	47.3 %
Aerospace and defense (28)	42.0 %
Travel and transport (49)	41.6 %
Financial services (84)	39.6 %
Energy companies (82)	38.7 %
Construction (45)	37.6 %
Forest products and packaging (40)	37.2 %
Electric utilities (67)	37.1 %
Food drink and tobacco (61)	35.3 %
Metals (48)	35.0 %
Consumer nondurables (55)	33.4 %
Retailing (125)	32.8 %
Consumer durables (82)	30.8 %
Electrical and heavy equipment (13)	30.0 %
Entertainment and information (48)	29.1 %
Chemicals (57)	28.9 %
Health care and drugs (82)	26.3 %
Business and industrial services (66)	24.3 %
Computers and communications (103)	18.4 %
Insurance (75)	18.4 %

From *Forbes Magazine*, January 1, 1996, pp. 234, 237.

■ MANAGEMENT OF WORKING CAPITAL

Let's turn our attention now to the "current" portion of the balance sheet, called *working capital*—the difference between current assets and current liabilities. Working capital can be measured using the "current ratio" (current assets divided by current liabilities), or the "quick" or "acid test ratio" (current assets less inventory divided by current liabilities).

Working capital has traditionally been considered a positive component of the balance sheet: A higher ratio of assets to liabilities was considered good performance. For example, $2 million of assets compared to $1 million of liabilities is a current ratio of 2:1. If assets were $3 million, the current ratio would be 3:1, in times past a preferable result. This preference has come primarily from lenders, who see working capital as money that can be used to repay debts and lines of bank credit. Bankers are trained to look at financial ratios and demand numbers that exceed pre-set standards. Dun & Bradstreet ratios show first quartile, median, and third quartile results; supposedly, any company with a ratio lying outside of the interquartile range—the first through third quartiles—is considered unsatisfactory and in need of additional investigation. Banks have often forced a company to borrow in order to put more cash on the balance sheet (and to increase the bank's loan portfolio!).

The newer view is that working capital is a drag on financial performance and therefore undesirable. Current assets that don't contribute to return-on-assets or return-on-equity hinder the performance of the company and may hide obsolete inventory that may not be salable or receivables that may not be collectible. The emphasis now is on reducing current asset accounts and funding current liabilities entirely from the ongoing operations of the business; that is, cash collected from sales is used for payables and payroll, with only a minimum amount left idle in the current assets account.

In the next few pages we'll examine reengineering opportunities for current asset accounts through both internal improvements and outsourcing.

Standard Receivables

Cash comes from invoices (receivables) being paid or from assets being sold. Normally, receivables are paid based on established credit terms. Strategies to improve the payment process include factoring, collateralization, and asset-based lending.

■ *Factoring.* Faced with the costs of credit, collections, the credit review process, and bad debt expenses, some small and medium-sized businesses opt to outsource their entire collection process to a *factor.* Factors buy accounts receivable and assume the risk of collection.

The factor reviews the creditworthiness of prospective buyers and determines the likelihood that payment will be made. When a buyer is accepted, the factor pays the selling company 96 to 97% of the cost of the product being sold. The factor then collects 100% of the sales amount directly from the buyer, pocketing the difference (3 to 4%). If the factor advances money to the seller prior to the factor's receipt of payment, an interest rate is charged to the selling company, similar to a loan; it's prudent, therefore, for the selling company to draw only those funds absolutely necessary to operate the business.

Because the credit decision is made by the factor, his or her expertise is usually confined to specific industries, typically those with many buyers and sellers. These include apparel, furniture, and general retailing, although recent users include start-up companies, exporters, and companies in turn-around situations. The factor's review of buyers takes into account their payment history, their current financial statements, the experience of their management, and general industry conditions. The financing is usually extended without any provision for recourse. Should default occur, it is the factor who will be at risk; he or she assumes the loss with no expectation of compensation from the seller. Selling companies usually follow the decision of the factor regarding the credit status of a buyer, although they may in some cases decide to assume the risk of collection and accept a customer the factor has refused.

If the cost of factoring is 4% and monthly receivables average $50,000, annual fees would be $24,000. Borrowing an equivalent amount at 12% would cost $6,000 (along with some bank fees for the credit line). Thus, factoring can cost about four times as much as a bank loan. However, some significant expenses would be avoided in a factoring arrangement: primarily the cost of a credit and collection staff and bad debt expenses from uncollectible accounts.

■ *Collateralized receivables.* In this program, a package of receivables is sold through a public securities offering or privately to a group of investors. The regular, predictable flow of cash payments for acknowledged debts makes the package attractive to investors. Although originally used with credit card debts and automobile loans, today a wide range of receivables are collateralized: equipment leases, health care receivables, health club fees, home water purification contracts, airline ticket receivables, even distressed (nonperforming) consumer loans.

Collateralized receivables are sold as a set of assets. If investors need an opinion, the assets can be rated by a rating agency (the majority of investors are insurance companies, which require a rating in order to assess their capital reserves against each category of investment). These ratings are usually on more favorable terms than the selling company would receive on its own merits. In assigning the ratings, investors and rating agencies examine the receivables history, with particular attention given to patterns of delinquencies and defaults. Many collateralizations are privately placed to protect confidential information such as customer lists and other competitive data, and in some of those cases no ratings are required. Private deals can be as small as $25 million, while a public sale as a security normally requires $100 million to be efficient.

With the market for public issues at about $200 billion, the interest return to investors has become competitive with standard bank lending. Initial costs are higher than bank lending, however, because of the additional professional services required: attorneys to prepare the public offering or private placement agreement, commercial and/or investment bankers to arrange the transaction, accountants to book the cash receipts and prepare financial statements, rating agencies to analyze creditworthiness, and income servicers to collect payments and remit to investors. Nevertheless, it's often worth the extra expense: Collateralization allows companies to transform a nonperforming asset into cash and to diversify its sources of financing.

- *Asset-based lending.* Rather than collateralizing receivables through a sale to investors, medium- to larger-size companies can often borrow against these assets. The business pledges the assets as collateral for a loan, and just as in factoring, the receivables are paid directly to the lender. Typical pricing is Prime plus 1 to 3% with various additional loan servicing fees totaling perhaps 1½% to 2½%.

Overdue Receivables

Inevitably certain receivables are not paid when due and must be aggressively pursued by telephone, letter, fax, and personal contact. An effective credit and collection program must be based on a well-coordinated decision-making process, using accurate customer and invoice information, strong incentives for payment, and a clear system of pursuit.

- *Customer information.* Good credit decisions can only be made when the information obtained on a prospective buying company is accurate. Along with the buyer's financial statements, credit bureau reports are important sources of data. The major credit bureau organizations include Equifax, Dun & Bradstreet, Trans Union Credit, and TRW Information Services (sold by TRW in 1996 to Bain Capital/Thomas H. Lee Company). Each bureau provides receivables management services, including debt management, collection of slow and nonpayers, check guarantee and verification, and risk assessment.

- *Invoice information.* Lockboxes provide fast feedback on uncollected receivables. Earlier access to payment information allows earlier initiation of the credit and collection process, and decisions can be made sooner about halting shipments to slow-pay customers. Delivery, processing, and cashing of receivables is generally faster with bank lockboxes than with businesses—as many as five business days, or one week, can be saved.

  The use of image capture lockbox technologies (as discussed in Chapter 6) is especially fast in recognizing unpaid receivables, allowing more efficient follow-up of overdue amounts.

- *Payment incentives.* Although cash discounts can be offered to customers to encourage prompt payment, the fact is that relatively few industries today offer such terms, and even fewer offer terms that truly appeal to customers. A manufacturing company client of ours with 100 major vendors showed only 15 companies offering any terms other than net (no cash discount offered).

  Terms of "1/10, net 30" means that the vendor expects to be paid by the 30th day from the receipt of invoice, but if payment is made within 10 days a 1% discount will be allowed. "2/20, net 30" means a 2% discount if paid within 20 days. The annual value of a discount to the buying company is frequently miscalculated in financial writing; the correct procedure is to multiply the number of "full payment periods" in a year by the discount. With terms of 1/10, net 30, the number of full payment periods is 18 ($360 \div [30 - 10]$); multiplying this by the discount (1%) equals 18%. Most financial managers would be fairly indifferent to this discount given that the average cost of capital would be nearly the same amount. A 2/10 discount—with an annual value of 36%—is much more attractive.

  Recent ratio analysis of the payment practices of American industry indicates that the average time to payment is not 30 days, however, but 45 days. This shows far less attractive results: $360 \div (45 - 10)$ times 1% = about a 10% value, with a 2/10 discount valued at only about 20%. In addition to this problem of marginal value to customers, there is often a problem in enforcing the terms of the discounts. For example, a payment on 2/10, net 30 terms mailed on day 11 (or 12, 13, or ?) is not officially entitled to the 2% discount, yet very few companies will demand that the 2% be remitted.

Still another problem with the cash discount is a concern by the customer that, once a pattern of early payment has been established, any subsequent failure to do so might be perceived by the seller as a sign of financial distress. Such a sign of "weakness" could negatively affect the vendor-buyer relationship, leading to changes in the prices and terms offered and the priority for vendor service and attention.

For all of these reasons, the use of cash discounts continues to decline.

■ *Systematic pursuit.* Through the use of specialized computer software, many collection systems have been automated in recent years. These automated systems help prioritize overdue invoices, with broken promises to pay and large overdue balances topping the list. Telephone dialing and letter writing, recording of debtor responses, and call-back plans can also all be automated. The use of automated procedures allows the organization to contact more customers on an as-due basis, improving DSO by an estimated 10%.

These systems are only economical to install in very large companies, however. Consequently, most of this work is outsourced to commercial collection agencies. These systems can provide the appearance of an internal operation, if necessary. Personalized scripts can be used for accounts that are late by a specified number of days. Daily data transmissions between the company and the collection agency allow each party to know the precise status of each account. Using automation, low-balance accounts and other overdues that might not usually be bothered with can more easily be pursued.

Costs for these systems vary by collection agency, and are often based on the number of contacts made rather than on a percentage of monies collected.

Maintaining current credit information on customers, carefully monitoring the receipt of payments, and contacting customers as soon as there is slippage in payment are the most effective methods for assuring the prompt collection of receivables.

Leasing Fixed Assets

Companies have traditionally owned critical plant and equipment in order to control the manufacturing and distribution process. The useful lives of these assets, however, have been dramatically shortened by rapid advances in technology and by improvements in productivity and quality control. At the same time, collateral "soft costs" such as installation, software, and training are becoming more significant. The competitive environment has forced many companies to acquire the new technology even though partially depreciated equipment is still on the accounting ledgers. This has resulted in book losses from the distressed sale or the scrapping of aging assets.

The pressure to "manage down" underproductive balance sheet assets, combined with the shortened life of technology, has encouraged financial managers to consider leasing instead of ownership. In a leasing arrangement, the asset is off the balance sheet, little or no cash is used to initiate the transaction, and the duration of the lease can be negotiated to the satisfaction of each party.

A further advantage to leasing is that the lessor can write off the depreciation—if the lessee is in an Alternative Minimum Tax (AMT) status. AMT status limits the use of tax preference items, such as accelerated depreciation, to reduce taxable income below a level set by IRS regulation, now 20%. Being able to write off the depreciation could make the cost of the lease actually less than the cost of a purchase. In evaluating a lease versus buy decision, companies should analyze the after-tax lease payment cashflows and the after-tax benefit of depreciation, using present value to discount the cashflows. (This analysis would use the marginal cost of capital as discussed in Chapter 5.) When this amount is compared to the present value of the purchase price and collateral costs, leasing is frequently found to be a lower after-tax cost than a purchase.

The competition to write leases has driven down their costs and led to some fairly creative leasing deals. Because the leased asset reverts to the lessor at the close of the lease, interest rate charges can be substantially below normal borrowing rates. Floating rate leases pegged to standard rates (LIBOR, Prime, Fed Funds) are now widely available, as are more flexible payment schedules to accommodate seasonal cashflows.

Buyer/Seller Partnerships

Inventory is not turned into cash until it has been sold, invoiced, and paid for. It's the one current asset that doesn't lend itself to aggressive management techniques—except for such measures as the just-in-time (JIT) technologies noted in Chapter 5. JIT requires that the necessary materials, parts, and products be in the right place at the right time, on the theory that excess inventory means waste and cost. JIT is now being extended to the point that suppliers need to own inventory while it's awaiting fabrication on the manufacturing site, transferring title only when it enters the manufacturing process. The idea is that suppliers and their customers can work together to make the production process—including ordering, delivery, invoicing, and payment—as efficient as possible for both parties.

Working together like this is a fairly recent development. Traditionally, businesses viewed the vendor/customer relationship as adversarial, or in economic terms, as a zero-sum game where one party can advance only by an equivalent setback to the other. A major shift in thinking has taken place over the past few years, however. The optimal management of working capital is now considered a common goal in a kind of "buyer/seller partnership," a positive-sum game in which cooperation leads to the greater gain of both. The partners work together to exchange information and reduce costs, primarily by eliminating redundant data entry, float, payment delays, and paperwork.

Often a successful internal reengineering effort will spur these cooperative partnerships. When it becomes apparent that savings from electronics and automation can far exceed the savings from float or payment delays, major vendors and customers begin to think seriously about working together. Typically, teams from the participating companies will meet and begin to explore the problems each encounters in managing the sales/production/payment process, including ordering, product delivery, inventory management, production scheduling, and the remittance of cash.

One way cashflow partnerships can improve balance sheet management is by minimizing the financing costs of each party. This can be accomplished by shifting such costs to the party with the lowest ACC. In a situation where a vendor with a high ACC is selling to a customer with a lower ACC, the cost of that high ACC is included in the price of the product, either explicitly or implicitly; that is, the buyer is either paying a higher price or receiving a lesser product. If, however, the customer transfers his or her lower ACC to the vendor, both parties would gain. Such a transfer could occur by making an early payment in exchange for either a cash discount (explained under "Payment Incentives") or what is called an *anticipation discount.*

⇥ An **anticipation discount** is a payment before the net date, but not part of the cash discount period. An example would be a $25,000 invoice paid on day 20 under "2/10, net 30" terms; an anticipation discount of 12% would be taken on 10 days of early payment, equal to about $80 [$25,000 X 12% X 10/360]. The amount of the anticipation discount is usually negotiated between buyer and seller but is generally consistent with the ACC of the party with the lower costs of financing.

Remember, however, that any cash or anticipation discount offered to a buyer must be provided to all customers purchasing on equivalent terms. The Robinson-Patman Act of 1936 prohibits price discrimination and regulates price discounts and allowances. Prices and cash discounts must be equivalent on goods of "like grade and quality" unless there is cost justification.

■ REENGINEERING THE CAPITAL STRUCTURE

This chapter has explored cashflow reengineering procedures that help optimize the structure of the balance sheet and reduce underperforming assets. Outsourcing techniques include factoring and receivables collateralization to transfer the collection of receivables, lockboxing to speed the flow of invoice information, automated credit and collection systems to pursue late and nonpayers, and fixed asset leasing to avoid costly investment in plant and equipment. Internal improvement opportunities include the use of credit bureaus to provide customer information and credit services, asset-based lending to finance current assets, cash and anticipation discounts to encourage earlier receivables payments, and trading partner relationships to provide greater operating efficiencies to vendors and customers. Businesses in a variety of industries have begun to recognize the importance of these techniques in helping to restructure and better manage the balance sheet.

chapter

10

Risk Management

*Take calculated **risks.** That is quite different from being rash.*
— George S. Patton (1885–1945)

*We are all **controlled** by the world in which we live, and part of that world has been and will be constructed by men. The question is this: Are we to be **controlled** by accidents, by tyrants, or by ourselves in effective cultural design?*
— B. F. Skinner (1904–1990)

Organizations involved in cashflow reengineering are often concerned about the *business risks* of changing the patterns and procedures of their operations, some of which may have been in place for many years. Managers worry that outsourcing will lead to a loss of focus and control, or that internal reengineering may adversely affect customers, suppliers, creditors, employees, or shareholders.

What these managers often fail to appreciate, however, is that a considerable amount of risk is already involved in *normal* business operations. Risk is inherent in most transactions; it's so pervasive we simply don't see it. Carefully defining and categorizing risk is a necessary first step toward effectively managing it. Business risks can be broken down into the following categories:

- *Trading partner credit or payment risk.* A vendor's risk that a customer will fail to pay, or the customer's risk that credit for a payment will be withdrawn. (The management of these risks was discussed in Chapter 9.)

- *Treasury operation or fraud risk.* The risk of the loss or theft of funds (discussed throughout this chapter).

- *Bank settlement risk.* The risk that a bank handling your transactions will fail. This risk is monitored by various U.S. government agencies (such as the Comptroller of the Currency) and by credit rating organizations.

- *Information risk.* The risk of the loss of data critical to the operation of your business (discussed in this chapter).

- *Financial risk.* The risk of large losses from moves in interest or currency exchange rates when using derivative financial instruments.

- *System risk.* The risk of the collapse of the payment system, possibly triggered by some cataclysmic event. This risk is monitored by various U.S. and global government agencies (such as the Federal Reserve System and the Group of Seven).

The advantage of cashflow reengineering is that it puts the entire business operation—including activities usually ignored or assumed to be satisfactory—under constant, microscopic scrutiny by management. This is the essence of Principle X (discussed in Chapter 3): The job of management is the continual exploration of opportunities to improve the performance of the organization. This chapter discusses the two primary risks of cashflow activities—fraud risks and information risks—and examines how to be better manage these through both internal improvements and outsourcing.

■ RISK AND CASHFLOW REENGINEERING

Some configurations of production, land, labor, and capital will bring smaller returns than others; this is a basic risk of business management. The only rational way to deal with this risk is to continually analyze alternative courses of action and to select the one that offers the greatest return at an acceptable level of risk. If the risk-return relationship of a particular strategy changes, management must adjust its decision accordingly.

For example, a reengineering strategy may be to outsource the collection of receipts to a bank for comprehensive processing (see the discussion in Chapter 6). The decision may be based on economics (the bid price may be below the cost of internal processing), service and quality issues (the bank may offer superior service to that available internally), or it may result from other factors. In any case, having made the decision and adapted this strategy, the manager would need to constantly monitor the performance of the bank to be sure that the quality, service, and price are maintained as promised. Should any important factors deteriorate, the manager would take corrective measures, possibly even terminating the service if necessary. This understanding should be clearly stated in the original contract or purchase agreement between the bank and the corporation.

Managers may well question the logic of outsourcing a function if such constant scrutiny is required, especially when a customer, supplier, creditor or other constituent group may be adversely affected by a failure in performance. Business risk is always present, however, regardless of whether an activity is conducted internally or externally; the job of the manager is to monitor risk and manage it on behalf of the organization.

■ THE RISK OF FRAUD

Although the treasurer is officially responsible for safeguarding an organization's cash and assets, every manager who deals with cashflow should be aware of the risks involved and be ready to take action to manage them. One primary cashflow risk is fraud: An estimated 500 million checks are forged annually causing total losses in the billions of dollars.

The potential for check fraud increased recently when the Federal Reserve Board issued Regulation CC, requiring banks to grant quicker access to deposits—a maximum of two days for U.S. checks drawn on local banks and five days for nonlocal items. Increasingly, bad checks are honored by banks before they can show up as return items.

Our consulting work frequently uncovers incidents of fraud and theft. For example, an insurance company issued a check in settlement of a claim for $70. Using desktop publishing technology, the check was altered to $70,000. It was presented and cleared through the banking system, and was not found by accounting clerks until three months had passed. When attempts were made to contact the depositor of the check, he had disappeared, to no one's surprise.

Fraud can be prevented by implementing precautionary measures within the organization, and by outsourcing when appropriate. Our discussion of outsourcing and internal improvements to reduce the risk of fraud includes both paper and electronic transactions.

The Risk of Fraud: Internal Actions

Consider these internal actions to manage *paper* transaction fraud.

 Verify the vendors used for purchasing. Fraud often occurs when invoices are paid to phony vendors or to vendors who overcharge for their products and services. Every vendor should be paid from an approved list, a list that is maintained and changed only by a senior manager who is totally independent of the payables and disbursement branch of the organization. Exceptions should be rare and should require multiple approvals. The legitimacy of a vendor can be verified through the following methods:

- Require the vendor to provide a federal tax identification number
- Have a credit agency conduct a credit check on the vendor
- Request some basic financial data; obtain an audited statement
- Visit the new vendor's premises
- Ask the vendor for names of corporate customers and call those businesses to determine both quality of service and legitimacy

Use blank checkstock or safety paper. Companies often order up to a six-months' supply of preprinted checkstock. This inventory—possibly tens of thousands of checks—is usually stored in a warehouse area before being sent as needed to the check printing site (often a computer facility). During the time those boxes of printed checks are waiting in their holding bins, it's virtually impossible to protect them against theft. Anyone with access to the check printing or storage area can steal several checks from the middle or bottom of a box, and months may pass before anyone will become aware of the theft.

One alternative is to use safety or watermark paper (made from multiple layers of colored fibers) that scars or bleeds when it is erased or chemically altered. Another alternative eliminates the need for preprinted checks entirely: Inexpensive laser technology can print the entire check face, including the magnetic ink character recognition (MICR) line, on blank paper.

Secure signature plates. When large quantities of checks need to be written, a signature plate is often used to "sign" each check. Many companies fail to protect these signature plates when they're not being used, leaving them out on the check-signing machine or in an unlocked drawer. Signature plates should always be secured in a locked facility when not in use. And whenever possible, checks signed with signature plates should be wet (ink) signed, particularly those over a predetermined minimum (such as $1,000); this requirement should be indicated on the face of the check and made clear to the bank.

 Eliminate check signing by signature plate. Eliminate the check signing process to stop fraudulent use of signature plates. Either use printed letters for the signature, surrounded by unique characters such as Greek letters or typographical marks, or use a computer scanner to scan the signature onto the laser-printed check. Scanned signatures can be printed using various color combinations to make it more difficult to copy.

 Limit the number of authorized signers. Because the local branches of a bank each require authorized signatures on the checks they issue, large corporations may have hundreds of authorized check signers on file with the bank. A bank cannot verify checks when there are hundreds of different managers signing them; it will simply honor any check presented. An agreement should be reached with the bank to narrow the list of authorized signers. The list should be carefully monitored to insure that when authorized signers leave the company, the bank is notified and their names are deleted from bank signature cards.

 Centralize the issuing of checks. Opening bank accounts at each facility of your organization for convenience, cashing employee checks, or other reasons, should be avoided. All checks should be issued from one site under the supervision of a designated manager. Consider outsourcing the disbursement function by daily transmitting your payables file to a bank or vendor, as discussed in Chapter 7. The bank/vendor will convert each payment to the appropriate form (check, ACH, EDI, wire transfer) and include accompanying remittance advice.

 Work with local banks to prevent payroll check fraud. A major source of fraud is the cashing of counterfeit payroll checks on a city's large employer, either at local banks or at other popular check cashing establishments (such as liquor stores). Local banks and businesses should be given information about identification cards issued to employees, such as the position of the photograph, the color of the printing and the background, and whether a fingerprint is on the card, as well as information on the kind of checkstock the company uses. In addition, a telephone contact should be provided in case there are questions about whether an employee or a check is legitimate.

Secure over-the-window deposits. The physical delivery of a deposit of checks to the bank invites theft either by the employee or by an outsider. If you must have employees handle the deposit, be sure the employees are bonded. Also, require that the encoded and stamped bank deposit ticket is reconciled with totals calculated from daily receipt processing. And be sure the carrier alters the pattern of the trip to the bank: he or she should use different routes, go at varying times, and carry the deposit in different bags or satchels. The trip shouldn't be predictable to a waiting thief!

Secure access to areas where sensitive or valuable assets are maintained, such as finance, information systems, payroll or accounts payable. With access to the finance department, a thief can steal checkstock, or use your bank information reporting systems to do a fraudulent wire transfer. Access to other internal systems allows thieves to issue payroll checks or checks to phony vendors.

Separate finance and accounting responsibilities. Smaller organizations frequently have the same individuals open mail, deposit checks, apply cash to open receivables, pay vendors, and issue checks. This is becoming increasingly prevalent as organizations downsize. With fewer employees verifying each other's activities, there are numerous opportunities for fraud and theft. The best prevention is to force the separation of those duties, and to require at least two different employees to handle the receipt and disbursement of cash.

Electronic fraud involves wire transfers, ACH transfers, and EDI transactions. Wires are final, same day transfers; once they're sent from your finance department, they are gone. ACH transfers are settled the next day, and EDI transactions are *value dated*—to be released only on a specified date. These time delays allow some opportunity to stop and recall ACHs and EDIs after the transaction has been made. For this reason, most security has been directed toward protection of wire transfers; for example, most wire systems contain multiple levels of security, including initiation, verification, and release.

Until recently, ACH and EDI transfers took place within a "closed loop"; that is, mainframe computer systems created ACH transaction tapes, which were then couriered or transmitted to the bank. Today, however, many banks conduct ACH/EDI transfers on personal computers; this allows greater flexibility but vastly increases the opportunity for fraud.

Consider these internal actions to help manage *electronic* transaction fraud.

 Establish physical controls on the computers used for wires and ACH/EDI transfers. Do not allow any more access to these terminals than you would to pre-printed checkstock. Secure the terminals to their desks by locking devices; restrict access to the work area where the equipment is housed; provide lock-and-key safety for backup copies of the tapes and disks supporting the money transfer systems.

 Use access codes with your treasury systems. Passwords should be secured, and they should consist of a minimum of *six* frequently changed characters. Do not allow passwords to be shared or to be posted in accessible areas. Do not allow unlimited attempts to sign on; if you do, a computer hacker will eventually discover your password. Allow instead a maximum of three tries, after which the user is logged off and access forbidden.

 Consider prohibiting telephone or other manual wires because of the significant opportunity for fraud. Establish repetitive wire transfers whenever possible, using the same accounts and codes. If manual wires must be used, limit them to funds moved between bank accounts. Do not allow faxed signatures with electronic transactions: A legitimate signature could be pasted onto a fraudulent transfer request. Insist on "wet" (ink signed) signature approvals.

 Appoint a security administrator to manage user access. The responsibilities of a security administrator would include issuing and changing user identification codes, receiving test material, handling changes to the system initiated by the bank or by you, and assigning transaction limitations. To maintain a complete separation of functions, the security administrator should *not* have transaction authority over payment systems.

 Review all procedures involved in the transmission or delivery of data tapes or disks. To prevent fraudulent media from being substituted for the originals, require all movement to be in locked bags. Do not allow the courier to have access to the bag before or after delivery.

The Risk of Fraud: Outsourcing

Given their vast experience in securing their own organizations, banks and other vendors of financial services are expert at managing the risk of fraud. Most companies are unable to match their level of expertise and cannot afford the significant fixed costs and technology required.

The following outsourcing actions can help manage *paper* transaction fraud:

 Use positive (match) pay. Positive or match pay is a *daily* reconciliation service, as compared to the *monthly* full account reconciliation described in Chapter 7. With positive pay, an organization's issued check file—including check number and amount—is transmitted each day to the bank; as items are then deposited, returned through the banking system, and presented for clearing, any item that does not match either the check number or the amount is referred to the issuer for approval or rejection. The issuer normally has about one-half a business day to make this decision. This prevents the honoring of checks that have been pulled fraudulently from the bottom of a stack of preprinted checks, or that have been altered after being issued.

Positive pay works only when checks are deposited *for credit to the depositor's account.* If a fraudulent check is *cashed* (as a a teller's window), which may occur with a payroll check, positive pay will not prevent a loss to the bank and/or the corporate issuer.

Desktop technology has created the opportunity for forgers to scan a corporate logo and to lift an executive signature from an annual report or other public document. The company's bank account data may be obtained from a variety of sources, including simply calling the company and asking for the account number on the excuse that money is to be wired in payment of an invoice. Often gangs operate as a team on a single community, cashing the phony checks and then leaving town before the loss is discovered (see "Bank Fraud, The Old-Fashioned Way," *Business Week*, Sept. 4, 1995, p. 96).

In response to these frauds with payroll checks, companies are encouraging the use of direct deposit programs (see Chapter 7). Another strategy is to encourage banks to fingerprint or "triple identify" non-customers attempting to cash checks (a triple identification involves proof of identity through a driver's license and two credit cards).

 Have checks received by a bank lockbox. Theft may occur when checks are received in an office and a deposit ticket is prepared. This is especially true when the same individuals have responsibility for managing cash and paying receivables. Regardless of float issues, consider having a bank lockbox (discussed in Chapter 6) handle the entire transaction flow, with any check disappearance the liability of the bank.

 Set limits on wires and ACH/EDI transfers for each transaction, for files of transactions, and for settlement day totals. Software is available that can review a set of transactions and notify you if limits are exceeded. Positive or match-pay systems provide receiving banks with lists of authorized transactions to compare against an ACH/EDI file.

These outsourcing actions can help manage *electronic* transaction fraud.

 Consider encryption and authentication technologies to enhance the security of ACH/EDI transactions. Encryption scrambles data into unreadable cipher. Authentication protects against data tampering by detecting any deletion, insertion, or modification. Both technologies involve the use of algorithms and secret keys known only to the company and the bank.

 Investigate the use of smart cards. Smart cards require PINs (personal identification numbers), similar to ATM cards. Their access codes are frequently revised and must be verified by the host computer; transactions can proceed only if matches occur with the codes expected at that exact time of day.

 Encourage your bank to use electronic check present-ment (ECP) to speed notification of NSF or dishonored checks. There are two components to ECP: electronic cash letter presentment to your bank (versus the physical delivery of clearing items), and access to comprehensive databases of known bad check writers and closed accounts.

■ THE MANAGEMENT OF INFORMATION RISK

An often overlooked source of risk is *information risk*, the risk of losing data critical to the operation of a business. The loss of proprietary business data can have a huge impact on an organization, yet the proliferation of internal and external sources of data and the dissemination of this data throughout computers and files, makes regular back-up and protection difficult to control.

There was a time not so long ago when all internal data was generated by a single mainframe computer system; the integrity of data could be assured by simply monitoring access to the system. Today there are numerous internal data systems, including mainframe, minis, and PCs, some standalone and some on LANs (local area networks). In addition, companies now regularly use external data, including bank information reporting, EDI feeds from VANs, online purchasing systems, the Internet, and various other types of interfaces.

Exposure to hackers, viruses, accidents, and intentional destruction has increased significantly, and few companies have developed procedures to deal with the resulting information risk. There are, however, a number of steps that can be taken to help protect your organization.

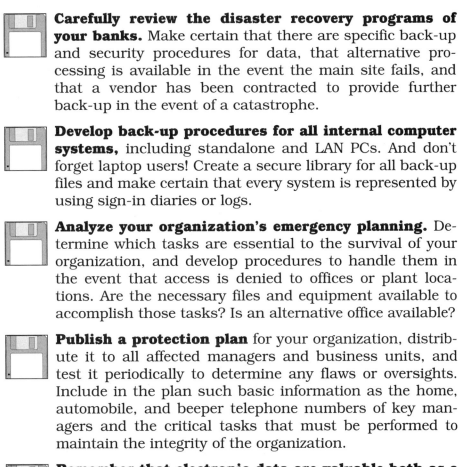

Carefully review the disaster recovery programs of your banks. Make certain that there are specific back-up and security procedures for data, that alternative processing is available in the event the main site fails, and that a vendor has been contracted to provide further back-up in the event of a catastrophe.

Develop back-up procedures for all internal computer systems, including standalone and LAN PCs. And don't forget laptop users! Create a secure library for all back-up files and make certain that every system is represented by using sign-in diaries or logs.

Analyze your organization's emergency planning. Determine which tasks are essential to the survival of your organization, and develop procedures to handle them in the event that access is denied to offices or plant locations. Are the necessary files and equipment available to accomplish those tasks? Is an alternative office available?

Publish a protection plan for your organization, distribute it to all affected managers and business units, and test it periodically to determine any flaws or oversights. Include in the plan such basic information as the home, automobile, and beeper telephone numbers of key managers and the critical tasks that must be performed to maintain the integrity of the organization.

Remember that electronic data are valuable both as a source of funds *and* as information to a competitor or "reseller." Most controls are designed only to protect funds, overlooking the possibility that proprietary data may be diverted for unethical uses. You should protect against both the theft of funds and the theft of information. Your banks should be able to provide information on security methods appropriate to the needs of your organization.

■ USING POLICIES TO MANAGE RISK

Along with internal actions and outsourcing initiatives, policies and procedures for managing financial matters should be developed and published. Policies and procedures manuals usually specify internal accounting rules, but only a small number of organizations have extended the process to other disciplines. Formal policies and procedures should be considered in several financial areas, listed in Exhibit 10-1.

A policy is a statement of acceptable levels of risk. The publication of policies (and the specific procedures for each) can help protect the organization from imprudent behavior or malicious intent. Compliance should be monitored and corrective action taken when necessary.

Derivatives Risk Case:
Procter & Gamble versus Bankers Trust

Managers have become alert to risks from losses on derivatives contracts. Some, like Gibson Greetings, Federal Paper Board, and Orange County, CA, have had major financial debacles on their hands. Corporations and governments have been seriously harmed by betting on the direction of interest rates through the use of swaps, "swaptions," other interest-rate contracts, and currency derivatives. A leading example was the dispute between Bankers Trust and Procter & Gamble regarding the financing chosen to replace an expiring swap: P&G claimed the bank didn't adequately warn them about the risks involved.

Derivatives are based on financial instruments, fixed rate debt, or floating rate debt (such as commercial paper or U.S. Treasury Bonds). With a "swap," two parties exchange future cash flows; for example, fixed interest rate debt might be swapped for floating interest rates (or vice versa). There are numerous variations of derivatives; some include caps or limits on the rates at which swaps can be exercised.

According to published reports, Procter & Gamble was presented with three alternatives, one of which involved a wager on the direction of both short- and long-term interest rates. The company selected a swap based on yields on Five-

EXHIBIT 10-1 Cashflow Policies and Specific Topic Areas		
General Policy and Rationale	**Subject of Policy**	**Topics Covered by Policy**
Liability management: To protect the credit rating of the business	Use of credit and debt capacity, including management of total commitments	Monitoring of borrowings Relationships with credit rating agencies Use of derivatives
Investment management: To establish guidelines for the selection and custody of investments	Statement regarding appropriate investments, including levels of risk, maturities, criteria for investment firms handling securities, and other activities	See the discussion in Chapter 8, pages 162–164.
Bank relations management: To specify responsibilities for interface with banks	Statement regarding managers responsible for bank contacts, including the assignment of specific activities	Establishing bank relations Opening/closing accounts Signature authorizations Monitoring bank quality
Liquidity management: To provide adequate liquidity for the business	Establishment of appropriate levels of working capital and short-term cash	Cash collection procedures Cash concentration procedures Cash disbursement procedures
Information management: To limit the potential loss of important data	Establishment of procedures to safeguard and recover data critical to the mission of the business	Internal and vendor disaster recovery programs Systems backup procedures Emergency planning Control of access to proprietary data Continued

---

EXHIBIT 10-1   Continued

General Policy and Rationale	Subject of Policy	Topics Covered by Policy
International transactions: To manage international transactions and funds	Establishment of guidelines to control the impact of currency fluctuations including exposure limits	Cash activities for international currencies Hedging currency risk International money transfer
Code of conduct: To publish an ethics statement regarding employee behavior	Statement on employeeconduct in accordancewith legal and regulatory requirements and corporate policies	List of situations that are inappropriate, illegal, or unethical, such as soliciting gifts from vendors or customers, trading on insider information, nepotism, etc.

Year U.S. Treasury Notes and 30-Year Treasury Bonds, even though internal valuations and the bank's pricing model were never disclosed. With the Federal Reserve boosting rates throughout 1994, the cost of terminating the swap rose over 14% above the interest rate on commercial paper, or a total of $195 million. P&G and Bankers Trust settled the matter before going to trial, with the bank accepting the largest share of the loss.

Two basic mistakes had been made in the transactions: First, P&G's finance department was used, not simply to pursue its inherent goals, such as reducing interest costs or exchanging fixed rate debt for floating rate, but to generate profits. Finance should *not* be expected to make target transaction profits. Second, Bankers Trust should have recognized that any financial transaction requires full disclosure of all pricing models and other elements used in evaluating the deal.

The Policies and Procedures Statement

In order to prevent such problems, organizations should develop and issue clear policies regarding appropriate behavior and acceptable risk. This approach is similar to that taken by many treasurers who develop policies for the opening of bank accounts, the execution of money transfers, and other sensitive matters. Any policy statement should include the following:

- A statement delimiting acceptable practice
- Levels of management permitted to commit the organization to specific levels of exposure
- Penalties for violation of the policy
- Responsibility for enforcement

Such policy statements should be distributed to internal staff *and* to investment and commercial bankers, with a signed copy retained by the issuer.

Of course, the degree of acceptable risk will vary from one organization to another, and no standard set of policies and procedures can apply to all. Some organizations, for example, will have a greater appetite for using derivatives. A policy on derivatives might look like this:

- *Rationale.* Treasury supports the strategic business goals of the organization and is not chartered to accept unreasonable financial risk.
- *Definitions of terms used.* A derivative is a financial instrument that is derived from another, more basic financial instrument, with the value of the derivative based on that more elementary instrument.
- *Policy.* No derivative contract may be executed that contains risk from the future direction of both short- and long-term interest rates or involves a level of exposure greater than ½% point (50 bp) or other predetermined level ascertained by fully disclosed valuations.

- *Authority to commit.* The following managers are authorized to commit this organization to a derivative contract: the Treasurer or the Chief Financial Officer.

- *Penalties for violation.* Any employee found in violation of this policy is subject to immediate dismissal. Any bank or vendor involved in a transaction in violation of this policy will be barred from doing business with this organization for five years.

- *Enforcement.* This policy will be enforced by Internal Audit staff, with advice from the Law Department.

While most organizations publish policies and procedures and distribute copies, employees too often have only a cursory knowledge of their content. To successfully implement policies—and avoid unacceptable financial risk—all parties should be required to sign a statement indicating that the policy has been read and understood. In addition, periodic independent audits should be made of activities involving risk to assure that the policies are being adhered to.

In summary, successful risk management requires that organizational policies be established, that employees and vendors be made aware of those policies, and that penalties be adequate to assure compliance.

■ TRIAGE FOR BUSINESS RISK

The management of risk is critical to the life of an organization. Businesses and governments have failed (or defaulted) when the necessary surveillance of risk has broken down and undermined corporate security. As we have seen, a variety of internal actions and outsourcing alternatives can be used to help mitigate risk.

It is prudent to assume that your organization will be attacked by fraud, theft, or system failure, or that a natural calamity, such as a flood or fire, will occur. It's possible—in fact, it's even likely—that at some period in the future you will be temporarily unable to conduct your normal business activities. Take steps now to assure that such a situation does not become a permanent closing!

chapter

·11·

The OPQR Paradigm

*It is better to know some of the **questions** than all of the **answers.***

—James Thurber (1894–1961)

*You're either part of the **solution** or part of the **problem.***

—Eldridge Cleaver (1935–   )

Exhibit 11-1 is a summary of the principles that underly cashflow reengineering.

Based on these principles, four overriding conclusions can be drawn regarding the management of organizations in today's business climate.

- Conclusion 1: The ***organizational*** performance or **"O"** problem.

  MANAGERS ARE REWARDED BASED ON THE PERFORMANCE OF THEIR INDIVIDUAL BUSINESS UNITS RATHER THAN ON THEIR CONTRIBUTION TO THE OVERALL PERFORMANCE OF THE *ORGANIZATION*.

  As we've discussed, managers tend to focus on their SBU's objectives or their own personnel needs rather than on the overall goals of the organization. While everyone ostensibly cares about the success of the organization, the more basic desire for most of us is to survive and succeed professionally.

  This attitude is analogous to the attitude of citizens toward the security of their country. In peacetime, individuals and groups within a nation tend to promote their own interests before that of their fellow citizens. Only when survival is threatened, as in wartime, are those individual and group causes subordinated to that of the nation.

- Conclusion 2: The ***process*** or **"P"** problem.

  MANAGERS DO NOT USE RIGOROUS METHODS OR ANALYTICAL *PROCESSES* WHEN ATTEMPTING TO IMPROVE THEIR ORGANIZATION'S PERFORMANCE.

  The pursuit of advanced education and certification has become universal in our business culture, with MBAs, CLUs (for insurance), CCMs (for treasury management), CFAs (for investment analysis), and other qualifications commonly attached to managers' names. These programs are academically demanding, and we are now in a world of highly trained managers. When considering a business problem, however, these same managers frequently choose the least difficult analysis. They draw the narrowest possible boundaries around the issues to be considered and use simplistic methods to analyze the problems.

\#\#\#		

EXHIBIT 11-1   **Cashflow Reengineering Principles**

No.	Statement of Principle	Example of Principle
I	*Managers often focus on objectives that serve their management roles but fail to serve the overall goals of their organizations.*	Issuance of invoices at Systems convenience; the "clean desk" syndrome in Payables
II	*Managers often focus on personal objectives that undermine the overall goals of their organizations.*	Sales below cost due to compensation plans based on sales volume
III	*Objectives appropriate to the enterprise may be inappropriate to the individual business or functional unit.*	Use of "profits" to evaluate business unit or manager performance
IV	*Evaluating a manager's performance by quantitative measures doesn't necessarily induce behavior in the interest of either the enterprise or the manager.*	MBOs as a measure of quantity (with no accompanying measure of quality)
V	*Benchmarking may oversimplify a manager's responsibilities, encourage haste in the workplace, and adversely affect product or service quality.*	Use of benchmarking without regard to the quality of business performance
VI	*A manager's reengineering plans should be evaluated for their impact both inside and outside the individual business unit. The evaluation should specify problem areas, methods of analysis, and other business units and/or managers with whom cooperation and coordination will be required.*	Analyze the impact of internal improvements vs. outsourcing of the disbursement process

	EXHIBIT 11-1 Continued	
No.	**Statement of Principle**	**Example of Principle**
VII	*Managers tend to focus on only part of a business problem rather than visualizing the entire problem and all its possible solutions.*	Redesign the payables system without comparing the cost of that redesign to outsourcing
VIII	*Managers tend to focus on either improving current systems or on outsourcing; the best reengineering efforts generally utilize combinations of both throughout a collection, concentration or disbursement process.*	The outsourcing of payables should be supported with internal improvements (by redesigning the system of matching purchase orders, receiving reports and invoices)
IX	*Managers who focus only on the* quantitative *measurement of alternative courses of action often fail to recognize essential* qualitative *factors.*	Qualitative factors not included in business decision-making
X	*The essence of management is the continual exploration of opportunities to improve the performance of the organization. The manager must constantly review activities by competitors and product/service offerings by banks and vendors, and be prepared to change his or her business procedures to accommodate new technology and new methods.*	

A good example is cash forecasting, discussed in Chapter 8. Does the manager thoughtfully analyze inflows and outflows to determine patterns of cash activity, perhaps utilizing statistical techniques? Or does he or she simply check the day's net position and invest or repay debt overnight? Most financial managers do the latter.

Every activity within a business organization is closely intertwined with every other, yet few managers concern themselves with how a change in their job or their division might effect other jobs or other divisions within the organization. For example, if the marketing manager decides to reduce prices in a product line, cashflow may decline, inventory may sell out, production may have to be rescheduled, and workers may have to be moved to different production lines. Were all these other divisions informed about the price change? In our experience, it's unlikely.

■ Conclusion 3: The **quantification** or **"Q"** problem.

ORGANIZATIONS USE SIMPLISTIC *QUANTIFICATION* SCHEMES TO EVALUATE THEIR MANAGERS' PERFORMANCE.

The manager's job involves a highly complex interplay of personnel, equipment, overhead, materials, customer relationships, financial results, information systems, and a host of other factors. However, when goals are established for the manager and his or her work group, they're based on oversimplified quantitative measures, without regard for the quality of effort. Typically, managerial objectives include the number of sales calls, the dollars of expense, the failure rate of a production process, or even more simply, the number of hours or days worked.

A good manager is involved in so many activities within the organization, with so many interfaces to so many elements, that a simple count of "successes" against a goal is laughable, if not an insult. What's needed is a more complex evaluation that takes quality into account without sacrificing objectivity.

■ Conclusion 4: The **reengineering** or **"R"** solution.

CASHFLOW *REENGINEERING* PROCEDURES HELP IMPROVE AN ORGANIZATION'S PERFORMANCE BY ANALYZING AND IMPROVING MANAGEMENT OF THE CASHFLOW TIMELINE.

As in Shakespeare's *Henry IV* (see Chapter 1), when managers focus on the "lifeblood" of the organization, their vision expands beyond the narrow boundaries of their individual jobs and work groups to the overall mission of the company itself.

The OPQ problems and the R solution are illustrated in the following cases drawn from our consulting work. Five additional short cases are included in the appendix to this chapter.

■ CASHFLOW REENGINEERING CASE: TELECOMMUNICATIONS COMPANY

The "O" Problem

A telecommunications company, comprised of independent, unintegrated businesses, functioned as if each unit was a standalone operation. At no time during our consulting work did any manager express a view of the company as a single billion dollar enterprise; they saw instead only the perceived needs of their individual business units.

Each business unit had its own sales force; its own order entry clerks; its own invoice, lockbox, and office collection procedures; and its own payment system. While there was movement toward a company-wide information system, most business units resisted this development and planned to maintain supplementary systems of their own.

The "P" Problem

We were brought in to consult with the finance department, which believed that a more efficient lockbox system could save the company about $50,000 in banking fees and float (as each major business unit maintained its own collection system). No one thought of asking us to review the cashflow timeline to develop an integrated plan of internal improvement and/or outsourcing.

The "Q" Problem

Sales representatives were compensated by the number of sales they made, regardless of the amount of the cash downpayment or the timing of remittances. The marketing of product was unrelated to the profitability of its sale—concessions were often given just to make the sale, with no concern for its impact on the ROE of the organization. For example, down-payments with orders were commonly waived, and late payments went without penalty. We recommended that the entire sales compensation system be reviewed, with an eye toward developing incentives to encourage earlier and larger cash payments from customers.

The "R" Solution

At the time of our consultation, each business unit was issuing invoices that included its own office and lockbox ("remit to") addresses, as well as the buyer's shipping and billing addresses. We recommended that, in the initial phase of reengineering, individual business units continue to handle invoicing, but that lockboxing and cash application be managed by one central collections unit. The intention was to improve collection float, reduce the total number of lockboxes and their cost, reduce the number of personnel assigned to the cash application process, and manage credit and collections more aggressively. The annual benefit was expected to exceed $325,000 annually:

Float:	One-third to one-fourth saved per day; assuming $2 million/business day at a 10% cost of capital, total savings would be $60,000.
Banking costs:	85,000 items processed at about $1.00 all-in, saving $100,000.
Personnel costs:	One-third of the cash application personnel in 15 business units at $25,000/year (salary and benefits), saving $125,000.
Credit and collections:	Savings to be determined, but certainly to be in excess of $25,000/year.
Balances in payment of bank services:	At two banks, saving $17,500/year.

In the second phase of reengineering, all invoicing activities would be centralized and the cash collection process would be outsourced (through lockboxing), with each business unit transmitting daily cash applications against an open receivables file. Credit and collection problems from late payers would also be managed by an outsource service in order to make the process more efficient and professional, and to remove the company from the role of collection "enforcer".

The annual benefit of these actions was expected to be an additional $175,000 annually:

Centralized invoicing:	Eliminating multiple billing systems saved $75,000/year.
Outsourcing cash application:	Eliminating maintenance of internal systems and receivables personnel saved $50,000/year.
Outsourcing credit and collections:	Eliminating credit and collection activities, having fewer lost opportunities (including float), and protecting goodwill saved $50,000/year.

Savings for the entire reengineering effort totaled $500,000/year.

■ CASHFLOW REENGINEERING CASE: PUBLIC UTILITY

A public utility providing gas and electric energy to consumers and corporate customers asked us to help them achieve an overall goal of improving customer satifaction. Unlike the telecommunications company, nearly every manager we interviewed described the primary importance of this service goal.

The "O" Problem

Our investigation of the company's cashflow revealed that several divisions within the company were conducting business without regard to generally accepted financial practice. For example, one division retained its own *shareholder services unit.* Shareholder services involve various stock and bond transfer activities and dividend and interest payment functions for publicly held corporations. Services include address changes and other file maintenance adjustments, dividend reinvestment plans for shareholders, quarterly and annual mailings, shareholder inquiry, proxy solicitation, the processing of stock option exercises, and the management of employee stock purchase plans. Banks offer such services at considerably less expense and with far greater expertise and technology than any individual company could provide.

However, when we discussed this alternative with the division manager, he reacted with hostility, immediately rejecting the idea. Based on our interviews and investigations, we concluded that the manager was interested only in perpetuating his job and those of his subordinates, with little regard for his impact on the organization.

The "P" Problem

Payments from consumers were received by mail at a central processing office or walked-in to *pay-station agents* (businesses in each town designated to receive bill payments, issue receipts and make bank deposits). Most of the checks received were drawn on a relatively small number of banks within the company's area of operation. Despite this, no effort had been made to open accounts in those banks so that customers could make direct deposits, which would have significantly improved cashflow. Instead, checks and currency received at both the central office and the pay-stations were held for courier pick-up until late in the afternoon each business day, well after the time for same-day crediting to the bank. Furthermore, no data was conveyed to the company from these sites; if it had been, financial managers could have more readily determined the cash position and improved cash forecasting.

The "Q" Problem

A public utility is subject to the rules and oversight of a state regulatory agency, often called a "public service commission."

To make any changes in its rate structure, the utility must present a request to the commision for approval. Insurance companies, securities firms, and certain other businesses face similar restrictions. This is because they either have a natural monopoly in the market, or are the custodian of customer funds—that is, serving in a fiduciary or trust capacity.

In reviewing the various activities of the utility, it became obvious that many procedures could be made more efficient. We found little interest in pursuing such improvements, however. Managers referred to the lack of a strong profit motive and to the fact that any costs could simply be added to the rate base and inevitably approved for rate increases to the customer.

The "R" Solution

The utility had not reviewed the cost of its check disbursement business for many years and was paying its banks in excess of 10¢ each for about 500,000 annual controlled disbursement items. This was such high volume that the price should have been closer to 5¢ or less; by merely changing disbursement banks the company could have saved nearly $25,000 a year in bank service charges. In addition, the utility didn't use the technology of larger banks, including services such as full reconciliation and positive pay. And although over half of the utility's vendors were from other states, there was no float benefit from the disbursement bank.

We recommended that disbursements be either completely outsourced, with all checks and electronic payments handled by a bank/vendor, or that at least the check disbursement portion be bid by banks. Key points in the decision process were:

- *Vendor pricing vs. internal costs.* The internal costs of disbursing, including all equipment, personnel, systems, postage and banking costs, were approximately $1.30 per item, which is consistent with the costs incurred by other organizations with equivalent disbursement volume. Bids from banks and vendors were significantly lower than that figure, some by as much as half. Banks and vendors also offered important services that were not currently used by the utility, such as full account reconciliation. If the outsourcing strategy were implemented, three positions would be eliminated.

- *Timing of check release.* If payment files were sent to the bank by midday, checks could be mailed the following day. This would assure that vendors would be paid within three days of the transmission of the file.

- *Special handling.* The vendor could provide special handling, such as returning items for attachments or delivery to vendors; adding checks written in branch locations to the issued file (for reconciliation purposes); handling checks being escheated (such as checks for rate refunds) and checks in currencies other than U.S. dollars. (*Escheatment* rules require certain regulated companies to remit uncashed checks to the state where the business is located after a reasonable period of time, usually six years.)

- *EDI.* The vendor offered to help the utiltiy shift from check payments to an EDI system. In addition to significant EDI experience, they offered programs for vendor enrollment and implementation.

The annual benefit of these actions was expected to be $250,000 in savings:

Outsourcing disbursements:	Bank service saved $250,000 a year and improved disbursement service.
Other:	Unspecified investment in EDI technology was avoided.

Both the telecommunications company and the public utility each realized savings in the hundreds of thousands of dollars per year. The total downsizing impact was significantly less onerous than those that have been reported in the press in recent years; the two companies in these examples eliminated only four full-time positions for each idea discussed.

■ PROSPECTS FOR INTERNAL IMPROVEMENTS

Reengineering should utilize technology to eliminate manual and mechanical processing wherever feasible. In addition to cost savings, automation makes data more accessibile for immediate analysis and decision making. For example, the cash position can be readily measured to schedule payments and settlements, and to optimize the organization's cashflow.

Many internal improvement opportunities will be highly technology dependent, particularly because so many organizations are operating computer systems that were installed in the 1970s and 1980s, in languages (such as COBOL) no longer supported by their developers. Because of the many fixes and changes made by programmers and analysts (most of whom have long since departed), documentation of these systems is often inadequate. This will be a particular problem as the century dating issue becomes more apparent with the approach of the year 2000. Many systems that compare or use dates in computations cannot comprehend a date in the twenty-first century.

Automation can be immensely helpful, yet many internal improvements can be made that do not involve technology:

- Move collection/disbursement processing from sites with the most expensive processing costs to the sites that are least expensive. Savings could be gained in reduced equipment, labor, overhead, and banking costs.

- Pick up mail in the morning as soon as it's available from the post office. This will give you more time for office processing and allow you to deposit received cash before the bank close of business (and before the ledger credit deadline).

- Renegotiate bank fees. Many banks currently have capacity, and many smaller banks are moving into cash management services.

- Charge clients for returns/redeposits in order to recoup bank fees incurred on NSF ("not sufficient funds") items.

- Allow your lockboxes to expedite the processing of exceptions. High exception rates add significantly to bank charges.

- Verify with Systems that your ACHs are completed one day after the date of the file transmission to your ACH bank. You can lose days of float when banks warehouse ACH items for processing on a future date.

- Have mailroom staff review post office procedures, particularly if post office boxes are used. Post office boxes may require up to three sorts; in busy post offices, mail may be held for one to two days. Use bar coding and preprinted return envelopes using lockboxes.

- Ask Internal Audit and senior management to insist that checks be mailed immediately after printing, with the stuffing of remittance documents by only a limited number of designated personnel. Organizations may be protecting one portion of the receipt and disbursement cycle while ignoring other portions. For example, they may use safety paper for the laser printing of checks (including the MICR line), but then return those checks to the business units prior to mailing.

- Rather than using wire transfers or checks, use the ACH to make repayments and to drawdown lines of credit from your banks.

■ PROSPECTS FOR OUTSOURCING

The recent trend to outsourcing has been spurred in large part by the proliferation of low-cost bank/vendor offerings. List price increases have been falling every year since 1991, with some 20% of all list prices discounted to corporations. The current era of overcapacity and discount pricing will end, however; banks and vendors cannot indefinitely price at or near marginal cost merely to buy business. With profits from corporate cash management services declining, new commitments to major investments in technology will be very carefully examined. Eventually, pricing will reflect a more rational calculation of required returns.

It's likely that outsourcing services will radiate from traditional banking activities, which focus on the central portion of the cashflow timeline—the depositing, concentrating, investing, and disbursing of cash. As we've noted, banks and vendors already offer various "comprehensive" collection and disbursing services: applying cash to open receivables; paying disbursements with accompanying remittance detail; and outsourcing payroll, including check issuance, direct deposits, and tax filing.

Companies in the Fortune 25 (or their nonprofit equivalents) are usually best off focusing their reengineering efforts on internal improvements, although outsourcing collections through lockboxing should certainly be considered. For organizations below that gigantic size, outsourcing can usually be justified for all of the cash activities we've discussed. The major banks have not widely marketed their services to smaller companies; perhaps they believe that the potential profitability—with small transaction volumes and sometimes less than investment grade credit—is too limited. Smaller companies do not "shop" cash services, however, and they pay list price. Community banks are beginning to aggressively pursue these customers, either through their own or through private labelled services. (A "private label" cash management service is usually provided by an established major bank or vendor, but sold to a customer under the smaller bank's label or name).

Future outsourcing services will likely include activities even further removed from the center of the timeline, such as the following:

- Sales data integration and review, and credit approval (based on transmissions from field offices or sales personnel)

- Issuance of customer invoices (based on a daily file transmission from the company regarding shipped orders or services provided)

- Credit and collection activities to slow/no payers (based on data regarding funds received and applied)

- Analysis of marketing activities, including sales, advertising, and promotions (based on analyses of company and industry data)

- Receivables financing, or "factoring" (based on orders received and approved) with funds collected as invoices are paid

- Inventory financing (as matched against orders received and approved)

- Management of purchasing cycle data (based on a daily file transmission from the company) including issuing purchase orders, matching against receiving reports and vendor invoices, and payment of those invoices

- Purchasing decisions, including the selection of vendors and the solicitation of bids (based on specifications and other data established by the company)

These solutions cross corporate divisional lines and require skills from nearly every discipline in the company. The financial manager's job is to ask the right questions, suggest possible avenues of investigation, and provide analytical skills in the search for answers.

■ PROSPECTS FOR THE ORGANIZATION

Successful cashflow reengineering requires an organizational simplicity that is responsive to the demands of the market. Organizations have tried the various managerial formulations and goals described in Chapters 2 and 3. They tend to work best when they're as simple as possible: that is, with the fewest possible groupings and managers, the fewest possible bureaucratic approvals or reviews, and the fewest possible encumberances or limitations placed on decision making. For most businesses, this will mean some form of functional structure, the kind used in corporations early in the twentieth century and never really improved upon.

The major difference today is that the classic "line" positions, sales and production, must be equal partners with the "staff" position historically called *finance* (but really *cash*). In addition, there must be an equal partnership for sharing information, something that has occured in many organizations. We can continue to call it "finance," but the position must be accorded responsibilities for all of the cash activities described in this book—especially those now assigned to line management. Without this change of mindset and responsibility, cashflow reengineering is unlikely to succeed.

There are very significant opportunities for further cashflow reengineering efficiencies and improvements. Almost any organization can benefit, regardless of size. Whether the change is in the structure of the balance sheet or in the components of cashflow, the potential opportunity is huge. Admittedly, it is difficult for most managers to dedicate the necessary time and resources in this era of reengineering, outsourcing, TQM, and benchmarking. However, some of your competitors *are* probably making the effort, and if they become more efficient, their competitive advantage becomes undeniable. This period will not tolerate inefficiency or sloth . . . personal or company survival may depend on you and your colleagues being heroes.

■ ■ ■

CHAPTER 11 APPENDIX

ILLUSTRATIVE CASH REENGINEERING CASES

■ INTERNAL IMPROVEMENT RECOMMENDATION: REMITTANCE PROCESSING

The following observations resulted from our visit and observation of an Internal Remittance Processing operation.

- *Internal processing costs.* The operation is basically efficient, with an all-in internal cost of about 9¢ per item (costs of about $2.25 million for 25 million items/year processed), not including the check deposit cost of 1.6¢. The 9¢ per item cost is acceptable, particularly when considering that agent deposits are all special handling items requiring additional operator attention.

    It may be possible to bid the business to a bank or vendor at about 8¢/item to save perhaps $250,000/year and avoid current "fixed" costs of about $2 million/year. However, special handling and depositing of on-us items to the banks may not be attractive to an outsource vendor.

- *Mail handling.* Mail pickup and handling is efficient. A unique zip code is used, which allows the mail to be worked as early as 6:30 A.M. Return envelopes are bar coded, and appear to meet Post Office requirements for expedited processing. Furthermore, you are processing at a major postal facility, and it is unlikely that any location would provide better mail times than are presently being experienced.

- *Credit and collection issues.* An issue for further examination may be the sequence of processing, in that the Internal Remittance Processing operation begins with sales representative deposits and then processes residential and business mailed-in receipts. The current thinking is that sales representative deposits result in many of the credit and collection problems presently experienced, and so they should be addressed first.

However, credit and collection actions are referred to the regions for processing, and any time gained by prioritizing sales representative collections appears to be lost in the "hand-off" process to the regions. There is no authority to contact agents or any customers of ABC Company for collection, NSF or any other issues, all of which are handled by the regions. Holdover of checks occurs on heavy volume days (such as Mondays, days after holidays). This may be avoided by changing the processing sequence, costing several thousand dollars/year.

- *On-us availability.* The Internal Remittance Processing operation direct deposits to your banks for on-us credit (at approximately 5:30 P.M.), totalling about 25% of all daily deposits. Other important drawee banks are not similarly outsorted. In 1996, Bank A clearing charges ranged between ½¢ for on-us items and 3¼¢ for regional check processing center (RCPC) items, with an average charge (excluding transit items) of 1.6¢. These is aggressive pricing, and is unlikely to be improved if competitively bid in the near-term.

  It is recommended that on-us depositing be instituted for Banks E and F and for any other financial institution constituting a significant drawee point, including any savings and loan or credit unions cleared through the major commercial banks. This would permit saving perhaps 1¢ per item in check clearing costs and would result in same-day availability for each on-us check, worth perhaps $20,000. In addition, the timing of the daily bank deposits needs to be confirmed to assure same day ledger credit.

- *Investable balances.* Because of the sequence of processing referred to above, same-day deposit data is not reported to Treasury. Investable balance calculations do not utilize on-us availability, which results in those balances earning the ECR rather than the ABC Company investable funds rate. This is costing some $40,000 to $50,000/year, calculated as 25% on-us, times $12 million average daily deposit, times a 1.5% spread of the borrowing rate versus bank ECRs. Until such time as same day data is communicated to Treasury, forecasts should be developed of likely on-us depositing using historical data.

- *Lockboxing opportunities.* Various high dollar checks are directed to the Internal Remittance Processing operation, apparently reflecting statement instructions to certain businesses. During our visit several such checks were observed, including one from Company Q for approximately $50,000. Items in excess of $1,000 should be directed to a lockbox to attain one day earlier ledger and availability credit, and a study should be undertaken to ascertain the systems and billing issues relating to these payments. The value of lockboxing high dollar items could be $10,000.

■ INTERNAL IMPROVEMENT RECOMMENDATION: EARLY RELEASE OF ACCOUNTS PAYABLE CHECKS

Vendor payments are made as payment terms dictate or earlier, after the taking of all cash discounts. Many U.S. corporations are paying in 40 to 50 days regardless of terms, and vendors of ABC Company would logically expect equivalent treatment. Statistics provided by Accounts Payable indicate the following payment practices during 1996:

Dates: Invoice to Payment	Number of Invoices	Cumulative % Distribution
0–5	3313	2%
6–10	9761	8%
11–15	21168	20%
16–20	19191	31%
21–25	17191	41%
26–30	33028	60%

Dates: Invoice to Payment	Number of Invoices	Cumulative % Distribution
31–35	42209	84%
36–40	7393	88%
41–45	4274	90%
46–50	2513	91%
51–55	1220	92%
56 or more	13020	100%

Some 60% of all invoices are paid prior to 30 days, with nearly 300,000/year invoices paid early by an average 6½ days. It is recommended that payables be extended by 5 days, to 35 days, to gain 11½ days of float.

With payables of about $2¼ million/day for Divisions 1–3, the savings would be approximately $2½ million/year at a 10% cost of capital and would simply involve instructing Accounts Payable to institute the change. Divisions 4–6 experience payables of about $400,000/day. For the entire corporation, the savings would probably be in the range of $3 million/year if a mechanism were developed to diary manual payments. (Each additional day of delay is worth in excess of $350,000.)

■ INTERNAL IMPROVEMENT RECOMMENDATION: SECURITY ISSUES

There are various issues relating to the safeguarding of company assets, including concerns for losses due to potential internal (employee) and external actions. It is unacceptable practice for Treasury to allow the computer room door to remain open most of the day year round. Anyone could steal preprinted checks from the check inventory, and months could go by before the theft would be discovered.

Access to the facility on Main Street is not tightly monitored, with security somewhat lax in the lobby entry. Similarly, check disbursement security at other locations should be improved, including the arrangements for safeguarding checks at First Street for payroll and at Investor Services for dividend/interest payments.

Policies and procedures should be developed to limit access to bank accounts and money transfer to designated Treasury personnel, and for other issues considered sensitive by the Treasurer. At present, policies only cover check disbursements, journal entry and reconciliation, and similar matters.

Although there have been few instances of known theft, it is likely that ABC Company experiences the same degree of risk as other U.S. corporations, and adequate protection does not appear to be in place. Additional suggestions include instituting an internal security function and establishing a "hot line" for confidential reporting of improper activities by employees.

■ OUTSOURCING RECOMMENDATION: LOCKBOX

Availability has deteriorated during the past year by one-half day in the Bank A lockbox. Results are shown by quarters (Q) below; however, the decline from May to December 1996 is more dramatic, in that immediate availability declined from 55.6% to 25.9%.

Time Period	% of Checks Receiving Immediate Availability
2Q1996	47.89%
3Q1996	39.59%
4Q1996	30.29%

With a daily $3 million deposit, this is costing up to $150,000/year. It is troublesome to observe this pattern in that the customer base of ABC Company is stable, bank availability schedules normally do not vary to any significant extent over time, and Treasury staff is not maintaining close review of lockbox performance. While it is unlikely that the entire one-half day of availability can be recovered, it may be possible to regain half of that amount, worth $75,000/year.

■ OUTSOURCING RECOMMENDATION: RECONCILIATIONS

Many companies have their banks provide full reconciliation services, matching issued to paid disbursement items. ABC Company has bank statements sent to Internal Audit, which matches statement items to accounting entries and requests information on variances. This is time consuming and, in some instances, causes delays in reconcilement of up to six months.

It is recommended that Internal Audit forego this responsibility, and that bank statements and full reconciliation reports be returned to Treasury. A meeting with Internal Audit management indicated willingness to consider this change in responsibilities. It would then be Treasury's responsibility to explain and correct variations from accounting entries, which are almost always due either to keying errors by ABC Company or to miscellaneous bank debits/credits that were never entered, such as NSFs. Internal Audit would do spot audits of Treasury.

Appendixes

Appendices A–D are suggested introductory material for a request for proposal to be issued to banks and other vendors of cashflow services. These standard services are discussed in detail in Chapters 4 through 8. The four appendices that follow supplement the material discussed in Chapter 4, The Outsourcing Alternative. In order to provide a succinct explanation of the process of selecting a bank or vendor, it was necessary to provide brief examples of the type of material normally used in a formal procurement process. The material that follows is a comprehensive set of bidding and scoring materials for retail lockbox.

Standardized RFPs, published in May 1996 by the Treasury Management Association (TMA) and the Bank Administration Institute (BAI), include a complete set of standard RFP questions for seven cash management products: wholesale lockbox, depository services, controlled disbursement, wire transfer services, ACH services, EDI services, and information reporting services. Orders can be sent to the TMA, 7315 Wisconsin Ave., Suite 1250 West, Bethesda MD 20814; $75 for TMA members and $100 for nonmembers.

·A·

Request for
Proposal (RFP)

■ RETAIL LOCKBOX SERVICES FOR A COMPANY

A Company is restructuring its remittance collection system. The Company is sending this Request for Proposal (RFP) for remittance processing services to selected banks and third-party processors previously responding to our Request for Information (RFI).

This RFP document is comprised of seven sections:

Section 1:   General Instructions and Conditions
Section 2:   Bidder Information
Section 3:   Billing/Collection System Description
Section 4:   Questionnaire
Section 5:   Pro Forma Monthly Account Analysis/Invoice
Section 6:   Lockbox Processing Procedures
Section 7:   Supplemental Information

Section 1 describes the general provisions required in the purchasing decision for vendor services. Section 2 requests specific bidder contact information.

Section 3 describes the Company's billing/collection system and the types of remittances to be handled. Bidders are encouraged to develop "creative solutions" for processing this mix in a cost-effective manner. The Company is seeking remittance processing services at the minimum cost, but would consider adopting enhanced services that improve efficiency and/or effectiveness of the overall collection and cash application processes. Enhanced services suggested by the bidder should be priced separately from the basic services to allow the Company to assess the anticipated benefits against the additional costs.

Section 4 presents a list of questions that should be answered by the bidder and requests a description of the process flow and services proposed by the bidder. If the bidder is a third-party processor, the questions related to banking services should be answered based on any preferred banking agreements you have in place; the name and location of the preferred depository bank should be indicated.

Section 5 presents a pro forma monthly account analysis for the lockbox services requested the Company. It presents volume assumptions and categorizes costs in a manner that makes it easier for the Company to compare the product offerings of each bidder. Bidders should add additional line descriptions, if necessary, to provide a complete definition of the monthly cost to be incurred. Third-party processors should indicate whether their charges will be billed directly to the Company or through the depository bank's account analysis.

Section 6 describes the lockbox processing requirements for the Company. Please review this section carefully to ascertain that you can meet our requirements. Section 7 is a listing of additional information that should be provided in your proposal, if available.

Please submit two copies of your proposal, along with product brochures and other relevant material, by the close of business on May 19, 199X. Use an overnight courier, if necessary, to ensure receipt on or before this due date. Send your proposal to:

Company Contact

Section 1: General Instructions and Conditions

1. PROCUREMENT POLICY

Procurement shall be handled in a manner providing equal opportunity to all businesses, including woman-owned and minority-owned businesses. This shall be accomplished without abrogation or sacrifice of quality and as determined to be in the best interest of the Company. The Company shall have sole discretion to make the final decision on the award of a contract.

2. UNIT PRICES

Unit prices should be stated in terms of the units specified. The Bidder may quote on all or a portion of a quantity as specified.

3. BEST AND FINAL   All bids will be considered to be the best and final offer by the Bidder; updated or revised bids will not be considered.

4. PROPOSALS   A proposal must be signed by an authorized officer and/or employee of the Bidder appearing on the response. The signature represents a binding commitment of the Bidder to provide such goods and/or services offered to the Company, should it be selected as the most qualified Bidder.

5. CANCELLATION OF CONTRACT   The contract will be of indefinite duration subject to the Company's right of cancellation upon notice as provided herein. Cancellation of contract by the Company may be for (a) default of the Bidder, or (b) lack of further need for the service or commodity. Default is defined as the failure of the Bidder to fulfill the obligations of the proposal or contract. In case of default by the Bidder, the Company may immediately cancel the contract and procure the articles or services from other sources, and hold the Bidder responsible for any excess costs occasioned thereby.

In the event the Company no longer needs the service or commodity specified in the contract due to program changes, changes in laws, rules or regulations, relocation of offices, or lack of funding, the Company may cancel the contract, without further liability to the Company, by giving the Bidder written notice of such cancellation no less than six months prior to the date of cancellation. Similarly, the Bidder may cancel the contract, without further liability, by giving the

Company written notice of such cancellation no less than six months prior to the date of cancellation.

6. ALTERNATE BIDS

Bidders may offer alternate bids that are at variance from the express specifications of the proposal, and the Company reserves the right in its sole discretion to consider and accept such bids. An alternate bid must clearly describe all variances from the express specifications and must be submitted along with the primary bid in order to be considered.

7. AWARD

The Company expects to award this business by June 30, 199X. However, the Company reserves the right to reject any or all bids if it is determined by the Company that its interests will be best served by so doing.

8. ACCEPTANCE OF PROPOSAL CONTENT

The contents of this RFP, the proposal, and such other provisions or terms and conditions as the parties may mutually agree will become contractual obligations, if a contract ensues. Failure of the successful Bidder to accept these obligations may result in cancellation of the award.

9. RECEIPT OF RESPONSES AND BIDS

It is the Bidder's responsibility to ensure that bids are received prior to the date and time specified. This responsibility rests entirely with the Bidder, notwithstanding delays resulting from postal handling or for any other reasons. Late bids will not be accepted or considered except under the following circumstances: (a) bids received on time do not meet specifications, or (b) no other bids are received.

10. NON-DISCRIM-
INATION CLAUSE

In the performance of any contract or purchase order resulting from this RFP, the Bidder agrees not to discriminate against any employee or applicant for employment, with respect to his or her hire, tenure, terms, conditions or privileges of employment, or any matter directly or indirectly related to employment, because of his or her race, color, religion, national origin, ancestry, age, sex, height, weight, marital status, or handicap. The Bidder further agrees that every subcontract entered into for the performance of any contract or purchase order resulting from this RFP will contain a provision requiring nondiscrimination in employment, as herein specified, binding upon each subcontractor. Any breach of this covenant may be regarded as a material breach of the contract or purchase order.

11. INCURRING
COSTS

The Company is not liable for any costs incurred by the Bidder prior to the signing of a definitive contract.

12. CONFIDENTIAL-
ITY AGREEMENT

Bidder agrees to hold in strict confidence the information, materials, and data that are disclosed by the Company in this RFP or related to this RFP and that are not made publicly available by the Company or any subsidiary or affiliate of the Company or an authorized third party. The Bidder will not use any such confidential information for any purpose, nor disclose it to anyone other than its personnel assigned to respond to this RFP, without prior written approval from the Company.

The Company agrees to hold in strict confidence any information, materials and data that are noted in writing as "confidential" and disclosed by the Bidder in the response to this RFP. The Company will not disclose such Bidder confidential information to any other bidder to the RFP without the prior written approval of the Bidder.

The Bidder acknowledges and agrees that any information, materials and data disclosed in the Bidder's response to the Company RFP may be used by the Company for any purpose whatsoever with the exception of a disclosure to another bidder as noted above.

13. SUBCONTRAC-TORS

The successful Bidder will have no right to assign or subcontract its rights and obligations under the contract without the Company's prior written consent, which may, in the sole discretion of the Company, be withheld.

14. FINANCIAL STATEMENTS

The Company will not offer, nor make available, any financial statements for the Company, its subsidiary and/or affiliated companies, that are not publicly available.

15. BIDDER QUESTIONS ABOUT RFP

Questions concerning the specifications contained herein should be submitted, in writing, to the individual specified in the introduction to this RFP. Other Company employees will not respond to telephone inquiries or visitations regarding this solicitation by Bidders or their representatives.

Section 2: Bidder Information

Bidder's Authorized Representatives

Please complete this form and include it, or a reasonable facsimile, with your proposal.

Bank/Vendor Name: _____

Bank/Vendor Address: _____

_____

_____

Respondent Name: _____

Respondent Title/Position: _____

Respondent Phone Number: _____

Respondent Fax Number: _____

Alternate Contact: _____

Alternate's Title/Position: _____

Alternate's Phone Number: _____

Alternate's Fax Number: _____

GENERAL INFORMATION ABOUT THE BIDDER

1. OVERVIEW

Briefly describe your firm, including lines of business, total assets, credit ratings, organizational structure, etc. Enclose your 199X annual report; if not available, indicate expected publication date and enclose last annual report available. Describe your corporate relationship management team, including all individuals likely to be assigned to the Company should this business be awarded to you.

2. EXPERIENCE

Does your firm have any particular experience with, or commitment to, the Company's industry? Please provide a listing of current industry clients, including types of services and activities provided and length of relationship.

3. DISASTER RECOVERY

Describe the "disaster recovery" facilities and procedures you have in place. What type of standby/back-up facility do you have? If your disaster recovery facilities are maintained by a third-party service provider, indicate your guaranteed level of service. How long would it take you to recreate a day's activity? Describe any disaster experience in the past three years, including the resolution of the problem(s).

4. QUALITY ASSURANCE

Describe your firm's quality assurance program. Do you maintain quality standards for specific processing/bank services, including minimal acceptable and target performance goals? What specific quality measures do you monitor for lockbox operations and what are the target performance levels for each? Do you periodically publish a quality chartbook or other reference, and/or do you provide access to customers to quality review meetings? Provide analyses of trends in quality performance over the past three years, if available.

5. METHOD OF COMPENSATION

The Company intends to compensate its processors/banks with fees or a combination of fees and balances. A pro forma account analysis or invoice must be provided for *each and every service* included in your bid, showing the pricing of requested services including individual (unbundled) pricing as it would appear on the monthly analysis or invoice (see Section 5: Pro Forma Monthly Account Analysis/Invoice). An account analysis/invoice must be provided to the Company monthly.

6. REFERENCES

Provide a minimum of two references of current remittance processing customers, including names, addresses, and telephone numbers. Reference companies should be comparable to the Company in size of revenues and in a related industry. The Company reserves the right to solicit all references for comments about the specific processing/banking service and for general impressions of the processor/bank and calling officers.

Section 3: Billing/Collection System Description

COMPANY DESCRIPTION

[Description of Company's Business]

BILLING

The Company sends invoices to customers with each shipment, averaging 2,000 per week. Statements are mailed on or about the 20th day of each month, averaging 5,000 per month. Customers may pay either on invoice or statement.

REMITTANCES

Monthly remittance volume averages 15,000 items.

- Approximately half of remittances are statement payments, accompanied by a scannable (OCR) advice; about 80% of these are paid as billed (that is, the check amount and advice match).

- Other remittances are primarily invoice payments. Current invoices do not include a tear-off stub, but many customers return the invoice with payment. New invoices are being designed that include a tear-off scannable stub. Future remittances may include: one scannable invoice/one check, multiple scannable invoices/one check, nonscannable invoice(s)/one check, check without advice (may have invoice or account number written in memo field).

- Some correspondence (without check), prepaid orders (with check)

PROCESSING

Specific processing instructions will be established during the implementation phase. However, as a basis for proposal preparation, please assume the following minimum requirements:

- Pick-up mail at postal facility.
- Open mail, sort, and separate nonmatching items and other exceptions.

- Process matching scannable remittances, including MICR data capture.

- Process nonmatching scannable remittances, including MICR data capture, keying of payment amount, and encoding/endorsing check.

- Process nonscannable remittances, including MICR data capture, keying of invoice and customer numbers, payment amount, and encoding/endorsing check.

- Photocopy checks accompanying nonscannable remittances.

- Deposit checks to meet critical availability deadlines.

- Report deposits and availability to the Company daily.

- Forward media for nonscannable remittances, returned checks, and correspondence to the Company via overnight courier; bill courier direct to the Company's account.

- Merge data files and transmit all remittance data, MICR, and deposit information to the Company's computer.

OTHER

The Company is considering installation of equipment to receive and display transmitted images of the nonscannable remittance advices included with customer payments. These images would supplant use of paper documents for cash application by the Company, noticeably enhancing efficiency.

The Company is also reengineering its entire receivables process and would welcome any information from lockbox processors that could be of interest in this regard.

Section 4: Questionnaire

A. General Information

1. Describe the overall processing flow you recommend for the Company. Should two separate addresses/lockboxes be used to segregate invoice and statement remittances? (Note: Statement payments have a higher probability of including a matching scannable advice than do invoice payments.) Would you recommend transmission of image data for cash application of non-scannable remittances? Would you recommend outsourcing of the entire receivables process?

2. Briefly discuss the type of support services and the hours during which they are available to the Company for resolving problems and questions. Do you have customer service personnel dedicated to retail lockbox services? Are customers assigned to a specific service representative for all their service needs? Describe back-up support during absence of primary support service representative.

3. What is the normal lead time required to implement a new retail lockbox client? What is the normal lead time required to implement a change in processing requirements?

4. Describe the data transmission options available to the Company, such as protocols, transmission "windows," direct or through third parties, etc. What security procedures are used to assure confidentiality and integrity of data transmissions between the lockbox bank/processor and the client Company?

5. What is the earliest time at which the Company's account balances can be reported, including: Lockbox Deposits + ACH Credits + Incoming Wire Transfers – Return Items? If all categories cannot be reported on a same day basis, please explain.

6. If you utilize imaging technology, how has it improved your processing quality and efficiency? Do you store digital images of both checks and remittance documents? For what period of time? Do you transmit digital images to any of your clients?

B. Processing of Mail

   1. Do you use a unique zip code for retail lockbox remittances? If "yes," is it restricted for retail use only?

   2. List your daily (weekday, weekend, and holiday) schedule for post office pick-ups of lockbox mail.

   3. Is fine sorting (to lockbox level) performed at the post office or at your offices?

- If fine sorting is done at the post office, is a bar coded/specific size envelope required? If yes, please indicate the requirements.
- If fine sorting is done at your offices, can the 4-digit add-on number to the 5-digit zip code be used to fine sort among major customers? If yes, is a specific size envelope required? If yes, please indicate the requirements.

   4. Attach a copy, if available, of the latest Phoenix-Hecht Postal Survey reflecting your collection time averages for all Phoenix-Hecht originating locations.

   5. Using your most recent Phoenix-Hecht Lockbox Evaluator (or an internal bank/company analysis if not surveyed by Phoenix-Hecht) reflecting lockbox mail arrival patterns, please complete the following table by indicating the percentage of lockbox mail received for each pick-up and the corresponding deposit cutoff for that pick-up. Please indicate the time of day used to start calculating the cumulative percentages received. Please also state which study (Phoenix-Hecht or internal) was used to determine these figures. The following information should be included in tabular form:

- Pick-Up Time
- % of Day's Mail Available For Each Pick-Up Time
- Cumulative % of Day's Mail Available
- Deposit Time

6. What is the latest mail pick-up time for remittances included in the current day's deposit for same day ledger credit? What percentage of daily retail lockbox mail is picked up after this time?

C. Retail Lockbox Processing and Funds Availability

1. Describe your pricing structure for OCR exception processing (e.g., at what OCR read-reject rate does the client incur "penalty" costs? Do premium charges apply to all items processed or only those in excess of the penalty rate cutoff?). Is a premium charged for nonmatching scannable advice/check? Multiple scannable advices/multiple checks?

2. What is your average error rate for lockbox processing?

3. What is your normal retention period for scannable remittance advices after processing?

4. How do you compute the availability that is passed on to the customer? Is float calculated on each check processed? Is a float factor assigned to each account on the basis of recent experience with the customer's receipts, or is the float factor used for all customers based on an average? If a float factor is used, how often is it re-evaluated?

5. Please attach to the proposal the bank's current availability schedule. Indicate the ledger cutoff time on which the schedule is based. If you offer an accelerated availability service, what is the additional cost?

6. Describe the options available for processing remittances in foreign currencies and/or other collection items.

7. How do you handle receipt of nonremittance items at the lockbox (e.g., misdirected equipment returns, customer orders, etc.)?

Section 5: Pro Forma Monthly Account Analysis

Provide a pro forma account analysis based on the volumes described in this RFP. Show all relevant costs in your usual account analysis format, including account maintenance and other fixed costs, and all charges based on transaction activity.

The Company intends to compensate its banks by fees or a combination of fees and balances. Banks should show how fees are translated to balance equivalents and how earnings credits are applied. Non-bank processors should include depository bank service charges (e.g., deposit, check clearing, information reporting, etc.) based on any preferred banking agreements they may have negotiated with depository banks.

Please answer the following questions:

1. What is your standard contract period? For what length of time do you guarantee prices? The Company would prefer to enter into a two-year contract, with price guarantees. Would you offer such terms?

2. Provide the formula you use to convert service charges to balance requirements for compensation. What is your earnings credit rate for the current and past two months? How is the rate derived?

3. Are service charges the same for fee and balance compensation? If no, please explain.

4. Are pricing discounts offered at increased volumes? If yes, what are the standard volume "break points"? Indicate volume levels at which prices change and the adjusted prices.

Section 6: Lockbox Processing Procedures

The lockbox will provide remittance processing services to the Company in accordance with the provisions discussed in this section. The lockbox will open the envelopes, remove and inspect the contents. Items that match as to name, amount, and appropriate date will be deposited.

1. Name, amount, and date mismatches

   a. Payee with a variation from the correct spelling due to an error by the drawer (the maker of the check). No restrictions; the check will be deposited.

   b. Undated checks: The lockbox will date the check as of the date of receipt and will deposit the item.

   c. Postdated checks: Checks with dates after the date received by the lockbox, probably made so that the check will be held until that date arrives. No restrictions; the check will be deposited.

   d. Stale dates: Checks with dates well before the date received by the lockbox, probably made so that the check will be returned to the maker for a more current dated check. No restrictions; the check will be deposited.

   e. Differing amounts: Checks for which the written and numeric amounts differ will be guaranteed and processed by the lockbox. The lockbox should review accompanying documents to determine the correct amount. The check is acceptable for deposit.

   f. Missing signature: If the drawer is identified from the face of the check, the lockbox will deposit and process the check by affixing a stamped impression requesting the drawee bank to contact the drawer for authority to pay (e.g., "if unpaid due to lack of signature, please refer to maker").

   g. Paid-in-full notation: Checks bearing a paid-in-full notation or words of a similarly restrictive nature or some variation thereof will *not* be deposited by the lockbox. They will be separated out and forwarded to the Company's customer service center as an exception item.

   h. Foreign items: Foreign checks will be entered for collection. The company will receive credit upon receipt of paid collections, less all fees and charges. Written advice of amount credited to lockbox account will be forwarded with the lockbox documentation.

i. Cash/cash equivalents: No restrictions. Cash will be deposited.

2. Processing of Miscellaneous Correspondence

The following will be batched separately and forwarded daily to the Company's customer service center:

a. Papers or documents that accompany payment, other than scannable remittance stubs; these are classified as unidentified items for processing purposes.

b. Scannable remittance documents that have been altered, crossed out, annotated with changes, etc.; these are classified as unidentified items for processing purposes.

c. Envelopes that contain only correspondence; these are classified as exception items for processing purposes.

3. Data Capture from Remittances

A complete listing of data capture requirements is provided in Exhibit A-1, including alphanumeric fields. These data include the following:

a. The lockbox will capture data from the scanline of all remittance stubs. The scanline contains four fields of alphanumeric OCR (Type A or Type B) characters. The design and layout of the remittance stub will conform to whatever standards are required by the lockbox processor. The specific data to be captured includes:

- Customer account number
- Account number
- Payment due date
- Payment amount due

b. The lockbox will scan the MICR line of the check. The data to be captured includes:

- Check dollar amount
- Customer's check number
- Customer's bank transit routing number
- Customer's bank account number

EXHIBIT A-1 Format of Data to Be Provided to the Company				
Field	**Description**	**Type**	**Length**	**Data Source**
1	Batch number	Numeric	10	Lockbox processing
2	Item number	Numeric	10	Lockbox processing
3	Misc. number	Alphanumeric	10	Remittance stub
4	Customer number	Alphanumeric	10	Remittance stub
5	Deposit date	Numeric (mmddyyyy)	8	Lockbox processing
6	Payment amount due	Numeric ($$$$$$$$¢¢)	10	Remittance stub
7	Due date	Numeric (mmddyyyy)	8	Remittance stub
8	Payment amount received	Numeric ($$$$$$$$¢¢)	10	Check
9	Check number	Numeric	10	Check
10	Bank account number	Numeric	10	Check
11	Bank transit routing number	Numeric	9	Check
		Total	105	

  c. The lockbox will transmit information to the Company's customer service center daily to update receivables records.

  d. The lockbox will print a computer listing of remittances processed and forward it daily by courier to: *[Operations Manager, the Company]*

 4. Unidentified Items

  Payments received without a remittance document or with a document without a scanline represent unidentified items. In addition, remittances received with one check and multiple documents with different customer account numbers represent unidentified items. Also classified as unidentified items are: multi-check/single-stub payments, overpayments of more than $1,000, underpayments in which the amount paid is less than 95% of the amount printed on the stub, nonscannable documents that accompany payment and scannable documents that have been altered, crossed out, annotated with changes, etc. Unidentified items will be deposited and handled as follows:

a. The lockbox will segregate unidentified items into a separate batch.

b. A copy of each check will be made and attached to the envelope. Any nonscannable stubs and scannable stubs with changes will also be attached to a copy of the check. A total must be calculated for the batch and the adding machine tape attached to the batch.

c. One deposit will be made for all unidentified items, with the tape total equal to the deposit total. The preferred option would be deposit to a separate account, used to segregate suspense items.

d. Average unidentified item monthly volume: 5%.

5. Exception Items

All remittances containing a check bearing a "paid-in-full" notation or words of similar restrictive nature will be treated as exception items and will *not* be deposited by the lockbox. Also considered as exception items: envelopes containing only correspondence. Exception items will be handled as follows:

a. The lockbox will segregate exception items (i.e., envelope and its contents) into a separate batch.

b. All exception items will be forwarded by overnight courier for next day delivery to the Company's customer service center.

c. Average exception item monthly volume: 1%.

6. Remittance Stubs

All remittance stubs that are processed by the lockbox will be stored for 30 days before being discarded.

7. Return Items

Checks returned unpaid because of insufficient funds will be redeposited one time. If redeposit of the item is not warranted for reasons such as "Account Closed" or "Payment Stopped", or if a check is returned unpaid a second time, the Company account will be charged. Send the check with a copy of the debit along with the daily exception items to the operations manager at the Company's customer service center. For returned checks in excess of $1,500, the lockbox will notify the Company by telephone call to the operations manager at the Company's customer service center.

8. Mode of Delivery

The "mode of delivery" refers to the method by which remittance materials (including exception, unidentified and returned items, etc.), deposit slips, and lockbox reports will be forwarded to the Company.

Overnight courier (to be received one day following processing day): Courier may be selected by the lockbox as long as the courier can guarantee delivery to the Company by 10:00 AM and certifies that a computerized tracking system is used to monitor package movements. The Company prefers to be billed directly by the courier.

9. Data Transmission for Cash Application

  a. Technical Contacts: *[Applications Manager, the Company]*

  b. Transmission Contacts: *[Applications Manager, the Company]*

  c. Data Requirements:

   1. Batch number

   2. Sequence number

   3. Account number

   4. Customer number

   5. Deposit date

6. Payment amount due

7. Payment due date

8. Payment amount received

9. Customer's check number

10. Customer's bank account number

11. Customer's bank transit routing number

e. Baud Rate/Protocol:

28.8 kbs or 14.4 kbs v.32 bis

ASCII asynchronous transmission

X-MODEM, Y-MODEM, or KERMIT file transfer

f. Transmission Time Frame:

Time frame to be specified by the lockbox; earliest possible time preferred.

Preferred mode: scheduled initiating call by the Company to (in order of preference):

1. Lockbox service provider.

2. Neutral site (e.g., electronic mailbox).

3. Lockbox, with a call-back to commence transmission.

g. Additional Requirements for Transmission Records

1. Control records: Include assignment of unique file identifier to avoid processing the same transmission more than once; provide various control totals, to be agreed upon (e.g., total dollars, total item count, hash totals on account numbers, etc.).

2. Batch control records: Maximum items per batch to be specified by lockbox processor; provide batch totals for dollars and item count.

3. Retention of data: Retain data transmission records for a minimum of one week.

4. Back-up tape: Receipt of a copy of the lockbox's back-up tape is not required by the Company.

5. Disaster recovery considerations: In the event of a service disruption caused by a disaster at the lockbox site, the lockbox operator must provide suitable recovery options capable of resuming operations at a satisfactory level within 24 hours.

In the event of a service disruption caused by a disaster at the Company's customer service center, the Company will provide an alternative site for receipt of data transmissions and daily courier packages. The lockbox operator must be capable of responding to redirection requests within 24 hours.

10. Deposit Reporting

Funds will be transferred to the concentration bank via Fedwire.

a. Information: Lockbox deposits (ledger, same-day/1-day/2-day availability), ACH credits, incoming wire transfers, return items.

b. Frequency: Each business day.

c. Access method: Terminal and other options provided by lockbox (e.g., telephone).

Section 7: Supplemental Information

Please include information for the following, if available.

A. Product brochures

B. Sample lockbox agreement

C. Lockbox specific Phoenix-Hecht Postal Survey (mail and availability)

D. Lockbox specific Phoenix-Hecht Mail lockbox evaluator reflecting arrival patterns

E. Lockbox holiday schedule

F. Sample output from lockbox processing—lists, photocopy, etc.

G. Availability schedule (also include the accelerated availability schedule, if offered)

H. Sample deposit analysis

I. Cash application information

J. Lockbox and related service pricing schedule

K. Sample account analysis

L. Implementation checklist (including lead times)

M. Standard agreement/setup forms for lockbox and related services

N. Organization chart of the lockbox operation

·B·

Measures of Performance

Criterion	2 Points	1 Point	0 Point
SERVICE CAPABILITY			
Disaster recovery	"Premium" service contract	Service contract + own offsite	Own offsite or none
No. Lockboxes (L/B) required	1	2	>2
Outsource everything?	—	Can provide service	Cannot provide service
Lockbox implementation time	<4 weeks	4–6 weeks	>6 weeks
Transmission security	Call-back/encription	Sign-on security	Passive/none
Balance reporting time	<5:00 P.M. same day	5:00 P.M. (same day)– 8:00 A.M. (next day)	>8:00 A.M. next day
Image storage	>6 days	3–6 days	<3 days
Image transmission	Checks + remittance advices	Checks only	Unavailable
Zip code	Unique retail + unique wholesale	Unique for all L/B	Not unique
No. mail pick-ups: weekdays and weekends	>5 per weekday + weekend	3–5 per weekday + week-end	<3 per weekday; no week-end
Postal service (USPS) mail sort to account	1 pass @ USPS + automated @ L/B	>1 pass @ USPS + automated @ L/B	Manual @ L/B
Average mail time	<3.0 days	3.0–3.5 days	>3.5 days
Mail pick-up time @ 90%	<7:00 A.M.	7:00 A.M.– 9:00 A.M.	>9:00 A.M.

Criterion	2 Points	1 Point	0 Point
Mail pick-up time @ 50%	<3:00 A.M.	3:00 A.M. – 7:00 A.M.	>7:00 A.M.
% deposited same day	>90%	75–90%	<75%
OCR advice retention	>6 days	3–6 days	<3 days
Ledger cut-off time	>5:00 P.M.	3:00 P.M. – 5:00 P.M.	<3:00 P.M.
Collection of foreign items	—	Buy-in @ discount	Outsort for collection
QUALITY			
Credit rating	AAA–AA	A	<A
Industry experience	Substantial	Some	None
Quality assurance pgm	Extensive	Moderate	Limited
References	—	Satisfactory	Inappropriate
Dedicated service representative	Primary representative + team	Team	Pool
Error rate per 10K	<1	1–2	>2
COST			
OCR read-reject cut-off %	>5%	3–5%	<3%
Penalty costs applied to:	—	Total volume	Exception volume
Non-match; multiples	—	Not counted as exception	Counted as exception
Availabilty assignment	By item	By item; fractional or float factor	Float factor
Price guarantee	>1 year	0–1 year	None
% earnings credit rate (ECR)	>(U.S. Treasury Bill – 2%)	(U.S. Treasury Bill – 2% to 5%)	<(U.S. Treasury Bill – 5%)

Criterion	2 Points	1 Point	0 Point
Fee surcharge	—	No	Yes
Monthly volume for discount	<50,000	50,000–75,000	>75,000
Pro forma cost/month	Low bid – (Low bid + 5%)	(Low bid + 5%) – (Low bid + 10%)	>(Low bid + 10%)
Estimated collection time	3.5 calendar days or less	3.5–4.5 calendar days	> 4.5 calendar days

·C·

Summary of Selected Lockbox Data

No.	Description	Bank A	Vendor B	Bank C	Vendor D	Bank E
1	Credit rating	A	A	AA	AA	AA
2	Industry experience	5 clients	None	Not directly, but several in similar processing environments	2 clients	6 clients
3	Disaster recovery	Own offsite	Own offsite	Service contract with recovery facility	Own offsite	4 severity levels; own on-site, off-site backup
4	Quality assurance program	Monthly tracking by customer; 30 error types	Tracking against 12 categories; customer call tracking system	Track holdover, investigation, errors, productivity	Quality references sprinkled liberally throughout proposal	Processor incentives, corporate strategy, tracking/report card
5	References	Listing of various references by each bidder				
6	# Lockboxes (L/B) required	2 recommended; 2 and 1 L/B solutions proposed	1 L/B	2 recommended	2 recommended, funneling into 1 account	1 recommended
7	Outsource everything?	Yes	Want to discuss "Receivables Matching"	L/B only (not billing); didn't address statement production	Yes	Should be considered

No.	Description	Bank A	Vendor B	Bank C	Vendor D	Bank E
8	Dedicated service representative (SR)?	Primary SR + pool of SRs	Implementation specialist; L/B pool thereafter	Primary SR + team	Pool, but can request SR by name	Primary SR + primary L/B representative
9	L/B implementation time	3–4 weeks typical	8 weeks	1–3 months, for programming	4–6 weeks typical (transmission testing and programming are unknowns)	10–12 weeks
10	Transmission security	Download to customer in auto-answer; can accept dial-in	Can be encrypted (not standard)	Dial-up or auto-receive, with password	Dial-in or auto-receive available; encrypted password + audit trail	Dial-in or auto-receive
11	Account balance reporting time	Balance reporting at 6:00 A.M. next day	Previous day balance reporting in morning, same day at 10:30 A.M. + 3:00 P.M. (2 deposits)	Previous day balance reporting in morning; same day at customer's cut-off times	Same day L/B at 5:00 P.M.; previous day at 7:00 A.M.	8:30 A.M. same day
12	Image storage	"Image lift" check copies + internal; full L/B application in 1997	In 1997	No	In 1997	No

No.	Description	Bank A	Vendor B	Bank C	Vendor D	Bank E
13	Image transmission	Not available	Check image transmission to PCs on pilot basis	Not available now; testing in next release (1997)	Piloting whole-sale check image in 1997	Not available
14	Zip code	Wholesale + retail share unique zip	No unique zip codes	Unique zip for all bank mail; caller service boxes for L/B	Unique zip for L/B; most retail uses bar code sorters	Unique zip code
15	No. mail pick-ups	10 daily, 5 weekend	3 daily, 1 weekend	4 daily, 2 weekend	19 daily, 17 weekend	7 daily, 5 week-end
16	Account USPS sort (U.S. Postal Service)	1 pass at USPS, automated sort-ing at L/B	Fine sorting at USPS	Retail: fine sort by USPS	1-pass for unique zip, auto fine sort at L/B; USPS fine sort for other	Manual fine sort at L/B
17	Average mail time	City avg: 3.21 calendar days	City avg: 3.30 calendar days	Not available	City avg: 2.93 calendar days	City avg: 2.83 calendar days
18	Pick-up time for 90% of mail	8:00 A.M.	7:30 A.M.	1:00 P.M. (85% at 9:00 A.M.)	8:30 A.M.	9:00 A.M.
19	Pick-up time for 50% of mail	5:00 A.M.	6:00 A.M.	9:00 A.M.	1:00 A.M.	2:00 A.M.

No.	Description	Bank A	Vendor B	Bank C	Vendor D	Bank E
20	% deposited same day	100%	75%	85%	98%	87%
21	OCR read-reject cut-off %	$0.10 @ 6–10%, $0.20 @ 11–25%, $0.35 @ >25%	0% (incur additional per-item cost)	2%	3%	$0.12 @ 3–10%, $0.25 @ >10%
22	Penalty costs applied to:	Exception items only	All items	Exception items only	All reject items for the month	Exceptions
23	Nonmatch; multiples	Not considered exceptions	Premium charge of 2 cents	Nonmatch OCR @ no penalty; multiples incur $0.25 premium	Premium charge of 3 cents	No penalty charge
24	Error rate per 10K	1.2	1	<10 (customer reported errors)	0.6	0.8
25	OCR advice retention	2 days	2 weeks	Normally return to customer; can arrange 5 days safekeeping	Check image stored 24 hours	Images retained onlyduring processing day
26	Availability assignment	Per item, fractional availability	Float factor	Per item or float factor	Per item	Per item, fractional availability

No.	Description	Bank A	Vendor B	Bank C	Vendor D	Bank E
27	Ledger cut-off time	5:00 P.M.	6:00 P.M.	4:30 P.M.	4:00 P.M.	5:00 P.M.
28	Collection of foreign items	Customer preference; buy-in or collection	Customer preference; buy-in or collection	Foreign currency L/B custom service	Send out for collection	Send out for collection
29	Nonremittance items	Forward in separate batch	Forward in separate batch	Per customer instructions	Per customer instructions	Per customer instructions
30	Price guarantee	1 yr standard; 2 yr available	1 yr	2 yrs, with prices guaranteed	2 yr	1 yr standard; 2 yr quoted
31	% ECR	3.67% (4/96), 3.73% (3/96)	3.29% (4/96), 3.33% (3/96)	4.00% (4/96), 3.73% (3/96)	3.65% (4/96), 3.60% (3/96)	3.67% (5/96), 3.73% (4/96)
32	Fee surcharge	None	None	None	None	None
33	FDIC charge	FDIC pass-through, quarter end	FDIC pass-through, quarter end	Monthly ledger balance without adjustment	FDIC pass-through on ledger balance	On average monthly adjusted ledger
34	Volume for discount	At 20,000/month	At 50,000/month	At 100,000/month	No standard volume discounts	At 25,000/month
35	Pro forma cost/month	$16,000	$20,000	$16,500	$14,000	$14,500

No.	Description	Bank A	Vendor B	Bank C	Vendor D	Bank E
36	Pro forma cost/item	$0.43	$0.52	$0.39	$0.35	$0.37
37	Estimated collection time	4.2 calendar days	4.35 calendar days	4.70 calendar days	3.57 calendar days	3.54 calendar days

·D·

Retail Lockbox
Evaluation Scores

SERVICE CAPABILITY		Bank A	Vendor B	Bank C	Vendor D	Bank E
Disaster recovery	250.00%	0	0	1	0	0
# L/Bs	10.00%	1	2	1	1	2
Outsource everything?	100.00%	0	1	0	0	1
L/B implementation time	100.00%	1	0	1	1	0
Transmission security	200.00%	1	1	1	2	1
Account balance reporting time	200.00%	1	1	1	1	0
Image storage	100.00%	0	0	1	0	0
Image transmission	100.00%	0	1	0	1	0
Zip code	100.00%	1	0	0	1	1
No. mail pick-ups	100.00%	2	2	1	2	2
Mail sort to acct	50.00%	2	1	1	2	0
Average mail time	100.00%	1	2	1	2	2
Mail pick-up time @ 90%	150.00%	1	0	0	1	0
Mail pick-up time @ 50%	150.00%	2	1	0	2	2
% deposited same day	300.00%	2	1	1	2	1
OCR advice retention	100.00%	0	2	1	0	0

		Bank A	Vendor B	Bank C	Vendor D	Bank E
Ledger cut-off time	100.00%	1	2	0	1	1
Collection of foreign items	100.00%	1	1	0	0	0
Non-remittance items	100.00%	1	1	1	1	1
Subtotal-Raw	35	18	19	12	20	14
Subtotal-Weighted	44.2	23.6	20.2	16.1	26.6	15.2
Subtotal-Wt Adjusted	25.00%	13.3	11.4	9.1	15.0	8.6
QUALITY						
Credit rating	50.00%	1	1	2	0	0
Industry experience	50.00%	0	0	0	0	0
Quality assurance program	250.00%	1	1	1	2	2
References	50.00%	0	0	0	0	0
Dedicated service representative	250.00%	2	0	2	1	2
Error rate per 10K	250.00%	1	2	0	2	2
Subtotal-Raw	11	5	4	5	5	6
Subtotal-Weighted	17.5	10.5	8.0	8.5	12.5	15.0
Subtotal-Wt Adjusted	25.00%	15.0	11.4	12.1	17.9	21.4

		Bank A	Vendor B	Bank C	Vendor D	Bank E
COST						
OCR read-reject cut-off %	100.00%	2	0	0	1	1
Penalty costs applied to:	200.00%	1	0	1	1	1
Non-match; multiples	100.00%	1	0	0.5	0	1
Availability assignment	100.00%	1	1	0	2	1
Price guarantee	100.00%	1.5	1	2	2	2
% earnings credit rate	10.00%	1.3	0	1.5	1.5	2
Fee surcharge	10.00%	1	1	1	1	1
Volume for discount	100.00%	0	1	0	0	0
Pro forma cost/month	300.00%	0	0	0	2	1
Estimated collection time	200.00%	1	1	0	2	2
Subtotal-Raw	19	11.8	7	6	14.5	13
Subtotal-Weighted	23.3	11.7	7.1	4.8	19.3	15.3
Subtotal-Wt Adjusted	50.00%	25.2	15.2	10.2	41.3	32.8
Total-Weighted	100.00%	53.5	38.1	31.4	74.2	62.9

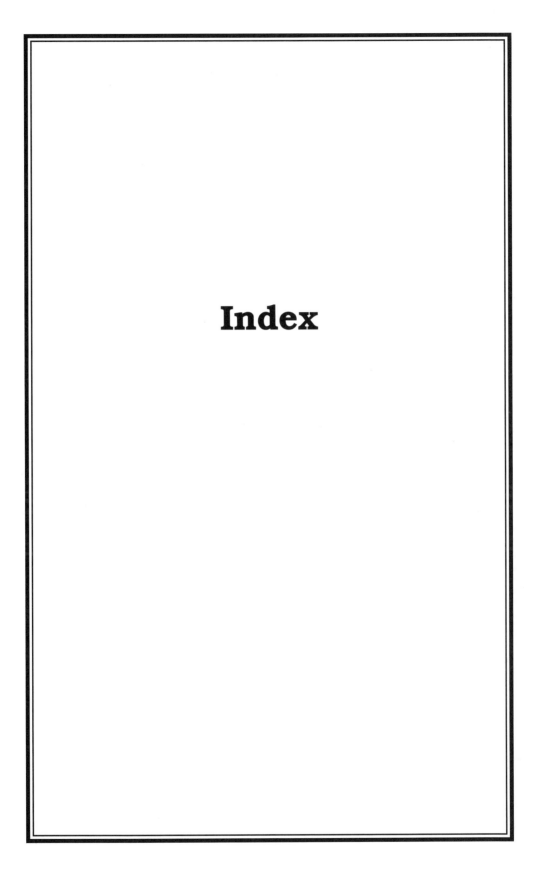

Index